ON BEING
BROWN

ON BEING BROWN

WHAT IT MEANS TO BE A
CLEVELAND BROWNS FAN

SCOTT HULER

GRAY & COMPANY, PUBLISHERS
CLEVELAND

Photographs on pages 86, 90, 103, 121, 126, 135
© Ron Kuntz. Photos on pages 112, 144 provided by the
author. All other photos provided by the Cleveland Press
Archive, Cleveland State University Library.

Quotation from *Burn On* by Randy Newman ©1970
(renewed) Unichappell Music, Inc., used with permission
of Warner Bros. Publications.

Gray & Company, Publishers
1588 E. 40th Street
Cleveland, Ohio 44103
www.grayco.com

ISBN 1-886228-31-0

Printed in the United States of America
10 9 8 7 6 5 4 3

This book is for my father,
and for my brother and my uncle Sam.

Cleveland, city of light, city of magic,
Cleveland, city of light, you're calling me.
Cleveland, even now I can remember
Because the Cuyahoga River goes smoking
    through my dreams.
Burn on, big river, burn on.
— Randy Newman, *Burn On*

The tragedy of life is not that man loses
but that he almost wins.
— Heywood Broun

Contents

Introduction ix

Brown 1

Cleveland Stadium 3

Orange 8

Things My Father Saw 10

"We always traveled first class"
A Moment with Lou Groza 16

1964 20

"It can't be just a bunch of guys in brown uniforms"
A Moment with Jim Brown 23

The Cincinnati Game 28

Brown on Brown
A Moment with Mike Brown 35

"We want Phipps!" 39

"I gave it my best"
A Moment with Mike Phipps 45

"I see what Paul Brown saw"
A Moment with Paul Warfield 49

The Pittsburgh Game 53

"For those four hours I hated my friends"
A Moment with Greg Pruitt 60

Red Right 88 64

Almostness
A Moment with Brian Sipe 73

Diaspora 78

Out of Town Brown
A Moment with Harold Manson 81

He Chose Us 86

"All I remember is being a Browns fan"
A Moment with Bernie Kosar 90

Browns Backers Everywhere
A Moment with Bob Grace and Jeff Wagner 94

Things Change 99

The Drive, the Fumble, and All That 103

"Three Disappointments"
A Moment with Ozzie Newsome 109

Autographed Picture 112

"No team will ever do that again"
A Moment with Otto Graham 117

Rumors of War and the Last Pittsburgh Game 121

Big Dawg and the Man in the Brown Suit 126

"Hundreds and hundreds of people openly weeping"
The Last Home Game 131

"It was just a spirit thing"
A Moment with Earnest Byner 135

Two Friends from Denver 139

I Have Raked My Last Leaf 144

The View from the Tunnel
A Few Words from Jerry Sherk 147

Acknowledgments 152

Introduction

THE PHONE RINGS, and it's my dad. We talk about the stuff we usually talk about—work, family. The usual stuff.

And as usual, we end up on the Cleveland Browns. I haven't lived in Cleveland for 20 years, and the Browns haven't played in Cleveland—they haven't even existed—for three years, but we talk about them. We always talk about the Cleveland Browns.

The Browns, of course, are returning to Cleveland as an expansion team in 1999, so now we actually have something to talk about: draft choices, the new ownership group, what the new stadium will look like. My dad has purchased insanely expensive seat licenses and plans to buy season tickets with his friend Barry. They'll buy three tickets, he says. One for him, one for Barry, and one extra. "Just like when we used to go," he says. That's right. It was one for him, one for my uncle Sam, and one for my brother or me. My dad, my uncle, my brother and me. We loved the Browns. We had to see the Browns. We *were* Brown. The Browns were our thing together, our time together in which nothing needed to be questioned.

Three tickets.

I think for a moment.

"How do you plan to split up the third?" I ask. Back in the days when it was just us, my brother and I had a system: usually, a coin toss for the first game of the season, then alternating choices the rest of the way. Eventually we started staging a kind of draft the day the new schedule was announced in the spring, with an elaborate method for weighting games—the Pittsburgh game was worth more, a game against some NFC loser was worth less. Michael, my brother, chose mostly on strength of opponent, opting to watch the Raiders or the Cowboys; I chose based on atmosphere, leaning towards November or December games when the sky would be iron-gray, the light dim, the air damp and cold.

"We just flip-flop," my dad says of the new third ticket. "Unless somebody has a special request."

I hesitate, but not for long. Something is stirring inside me—part of me still remembers.

Looking at my hand holding the telephone, I see the hair on my forearms standing up. Something I thought was dead, it seems, sleeps uneasily still. What will it be like when people crowd the stadium, after waiting four years, to be part of that again?

"So then, say, if I wanted to go with you to the first regular-season game when the Browns come back, I could request that?"

"Sure," he says, betraying no emotion. "I'll check with Barry. I'll let you know."

We say good-bye, but as I replace the phone in its cradle I am actually trembling.

Something is stirring inside me. Something I thought—something I knew—I had said good-bye to. The Browns, it seems, still own me.

A Browns game. When I was 12, a Browns game lived somewhere in my spirit between a presidential inauguration and New Year's Eve—it was the first true event I can ever remember, trumping weddings and bar mitzvahs, holidays and anniversaries in importance in my mind. I remember gatherings of men outside the catering halls, smoking cigarettes, heads bent over transistor radios, during autumn weddings held, recklessly, on Sunday afternoons. That was a clue to what was important.

The Browns were important. They may or may not have been important to the outside world, but they were important to us. They were something I knew.

I grew up, and I moved away, but they never diminished in importance. As I matured, and games and sports began to occupy a less central position in my life, the Browns always, somehow, claimed a special exemption. I left the Indians and rooted for the Phillies; I never paid much attention to college athletics; more and more I let my interest in sports diminish. Yet on Sundays my new life in Raleigh, North Carolina, stopped and I went to a bar and met up with dozens of other Clevelanders to watch the Browns fumble one away to the San Diego Chargers or the Cincinnati Bengals.

As I aged and as football progressed, I kept going, but I groused more and more. "I just wish the Browns would win one championship, so I could quit watching this damn game," I'd say, then head off to Chi-Chi's, for wings and *Browns News Illustrated* and tossing a football in the parking lot with somebody else's kids.

Then, finally, 1995. A growing breach between Browns owner Art Modell and the city widened to the point where Modell moved his team to Baltimore. Approached by friends as though I had lost a relative, I was philosophical. "Finally," I said, "I have my Sunday afternoons back." I had been ready to be done with football for years, as I saw it, and now, finally, I could comfortably no longer care. It actually worked that way. An NFL game comes on, I watch it, I don't, it's no big deal. I'm on to other things.

And then, they're back. A rumored expansion team materializes to take the place of the old Browns, now the Baltimore Ravens. Those Ravens, of course, took the place of Baltimore's once-adored Colts, who now labor in Indianapolis. The Colts' history traveled with them; the Ravens started anew, with barely a backwards glance.

Not so the Browns. When the old team left Cleveland, the records, the team colors, the history remained behind, waiting. And in more than just old record books and uniforms, it appears. Inside me, as inside almost every other old Browns fan I talk to, something is happening. The Browns are coming back, and we want them.

I don't take any action at first, though. For weeks I just go about my business, barely noticing that the Browns are coming back.

But they are. And somehow, for some reason, they haven't let go of me. As the days go by, I start thinking about that, trying to find perspective. Looking for the power behind this longing. What is it? Is it the Browns? Football? Organized sports? Is this some kind of religion, or is it some weird variety of civic pride—in a city I moved away from two decades ago? People talk all the time now about how much sports mean to us. Theories about why that is range from the decline of our Roman Empire–like society, to too much time on our hands, to the rise of sports as secular religion. I mull it over, and I start to get ideas. And more than ever, I want to talk to those other Browns fans, those other members of whatever tribe this is. I recall conversations—with people like Harold Manson, a guy I met in a bar, in front of a broadcast of an exhibition game. People like Brian Sipe, one of the few Browns I've actually conversed with.

I want to talk to them, because suddenly, for the first time in years, we have something to look forward to. Then one day the phone rings. It's my dad.

"You're on," he says. I almost ask for what, but he keeps talking. "For the first game. The ticket is yours." And it's true—finally, we're not just filling time with idle chatter about the Browns. This time we have something to look forward to.

We're going to a Browns game.

ON BEING
BROWN

Brown

Brown *is the color of my true love's . . .*

Start, naturally enough, with the ground. The ground on the field of Cleveland Municipal Stadium is as brown as dry, dead leaves, as brown as any ground has a right to be, as brown as any ground on which men play professional sports. On sunny days it is a yellow, sandy brown, but the first time I ever see it, during a dispirited 6–2 Browns loss to the Dallas Cowboys, it is a wet, muddy brown in a thick stripe down the middle of the field. The game is long-time coach Blanton Collier's final home game, and the uneventful loss means more than I have any way of knowing at the time. Collier is the last man to guide the Browns to a championship, but to me this means little; I am only 10, and I know nothing of history. And this is, after all, the first time we meet.

Brown is the color of the milky coffee that my father pours out of his thermos, steaming into the damp November air, and sips to warm up. At home coffee is a bitter beverage, objectionable to my young tastes; at the stadium, coffee bespeaks halftime, the closeness of my father and my uncle, a momentary lessening of the tremendous pressure that fills the stadium while the game is in progress. The small, acrid coffee aroma mingles with the other rich stadium smells—of beer, of hot dogs, of liquor, of men's breath. Above all, the coffee is brown.

1

Brown is the color of the crowd—a stadium Browns game is the first place that I experience the feeling of being in a crowd comprising many black people. To me they seem friendly, gentle, supportive in a deep, resonant way. They are brown; Jim Brown, something of a god in our household, is brown; the team is named the Browns. It all seems to go together in some inexplicable, mystical way, and I envy these brown people their more obvious identification with the team. In the distance, on the other side of the stadium, the crowd, a mixture of brown and white faces, gray and brown overcoats, and the white vapor of condensing breath, is the color of the coffee that comes out of my dad's thermos, and so the crowd becomes in memory warm and steamy as well.

Brown is the color of the unfamiliar downtown buildings we pass as we drive in to the game, always arriving a half hour before kickoff. Brown is the color of the factories we can see in the distance under the low gray clouds beyond the bleachers. Brown is the color of the leaves by the side of the road, the mud at the schoolyard where my brother and I pretend we are football players. Brown is the color of autumn.

Brown is the color of my true love.

Cleveland Stadium

THE TERMINAL TOWER is my father.

This is not so much a thought as a feeling that I can remember having, so young that my head does not reach to the window in the backseat of the car, and I see the ornate, almost Gothic spire of the Terminal Tower only by craning my neck as we drive through downtown Cleveland. I don't remember being surprised by the thought, and even now, though facile psychological interpretations offer themselves, I remember the feeling as one of simple acknowledgment.

There was the tower, strong, rigid, powerful: 52 stories tall and at that point the only downtown landmark of the city from which I had sprung, standing at its absolute center. From there I had come—there was my origin. The Terminal Tower was my father.

Only years later, as an adult, huddled among masses of fans in the gray, weatherworn double-deck horseshoe of pale blue girders and dusty slatted wooden seats, did I realize that Cleveland Stadium was my mother, curved and worn and gentle. Within its graceful swell I was contained, bound, nourished; there I fled self and became part of a community, a family of depthless emotion and profound support. There I felt the first embrace of a parent I didn't even know I had, became one with a tribe I could never leave.

The stadium was in every way family—comfortable, faded,

and not necessarily perfect but truly and ineradicably ours. "It's not a very good place to watch a baseball game, and it's not a very good place to watch a football game," fans used to say, "but other than that it's a great building."

Built in 1931 as part of an abandoned Cleveland attempt to make a play for the Olympics, the stadium was for decades one of the biggest in the NFL, though it didn't see much use until the Browns came along. The Indians played mostly in old League Park until 1946, when their fans started needing more seats, but otherwise, the stadium mostly sat empty.

And for good reason. Within its vast sandy playing area, the benches and ballplayers were rarely close enough for a player to hear a shouted comment, much less near enough for the fans to feel like they were part of the game. Over the decades, the stadium hosted boxing matches and rock concerts, Billy Graham crusades and fireworks shows, but mostly it was like the mother in a cartoon or a comedic routine—a little tired, left alone too much, wondering when its next visit would be.

And a mother in the negative sense, too. The Browns, struggling with their own internal demons, virtually alone among NFL teams, never within recent memory underwent a period during which they were unbeatable at home. Though gray and graceful, Cleveland Municipal Stadium was also huge, fierce, and unpredictable. What would Freud or Jung say? Like the mother in the great unconscious, it was a place to fear devourment as well as a place to receive support. The stadium giveth and the stadium taketh away.

In fact, analyze the Browns and their almost impossible latter-day penchant for shooting themselves in the foot when faced with their greatest success. Fear of success? Inability to pull the trigger? For whatever reasons, the Browns in their last three decades at the stadium were unable to win the game

4

that would shake them free of that gray horseshoe. Their last championship occurred in its encircling arms—before the days of the neutral-site Super Bowl—and it seemed loath to release the embrace to allow them to seek another. The Browns were a team that could not escape their home, could not cut the apron strings, and of such people psychologists like to say they have "mother issues."

Okay, I'll grant you, that's a pretty odd theory: You can't really blame a team's inability to make the Super Bowl on a stadium. But the Browns stopped winning championships just about exactly the time the NFL championship started growing in cultural importance, when the neutral-site Super Bowl took over. Thereafter they never escaped that gray countenance alive.

Of course, I'm not the only one who blamed some stuff on the stadium. After all, when Art Modell spirited the team off to Baltimore in 1995, the stadium was the only excuse he could muster.

This, to a certain degree, any reasonable modern sports fan could understand. Luxury boxes, concessions, parking, amenities: the usual litany of complaints emerged from the Browns' ownership, and most of it seemed true. The stadium was big, old, expensive, falling apart, and as fans had always said, not a particularly good place to watch an athletic event.

But to Browns fans, that wasn't troubling—that was charming. It may not have offered the best view of a football game— unless you liked close-ups of a pole—but it was a smashing place to *be*. We remember those dusty blue girders, those gray wooden seats, those men's rooms with their wall-length horse-trough urinals, the windows with the chicken wire across them, the wind whistling in through the aluminum slats along the back of the upper deck, the pigeons roosting in that skeletal girderwork that made the whole building feel as though you were under all of the vast bridges in the Flats at once. The Indians' new ballpark, Jacobs Field, has light standards that, reviewers say, are supposed to look like factory smokestacks. Old Municipal Stadium didn't have to evoke the feel of an industrial relic—it *was* one.

But inside you knew you were someplace. Looking out over the lake under autumn skies, you knew it was the perfect place to watch a blue-collar sport, a sport designed to be played outside, a sport whose strongest fans—in Detroit, in Chicago, in Green Bay—always seemed to be near the Great Lakes.

When I paid my last visit to the old Browns, watching them lose to the Steelers in their second-to-last home game, we noted, my brother and sister and I, that we were saying good-bye more to the stadium than the team. Uncertainty surrounded the team—they might not be allowed to move, an expansion team might come, a franchise might move to Cleveland and adopt the team name and colors—but nobody denied the obvious: if professional football was going to return to Cleveland, we were going to get a new stadium. This one was on its way out. The yellow brick facades, the blue girders, the poles that by making you twist in your seat to see all the action somehow made the game more exciting—all that was going away.

On the way out of that game I bought a pennant, which remains one of the few pieces of fan paraphernalia I've got. Brown, orange, and white, it just looked cool at the vendor's stand—I handed over my five dollars or whatever and took it along. It wasn't until we got to our car that I actually looked at the pennant. It's in Browns colors, all right, but it turns out to be a type of pennant I've never seen anywhere else. It doesn't have a helmet on it—the artwork is a line drawing of the stadium. "Municipal Stadium," the pennant says. "Home of the Cleveland Browns & Indians."

I don't know that any other cities have pennants commemorating their stadiums, but I'm glad ours did. I'm sure the new stadium will be wonderful—it's outdoors, it has real grass, it's on the same spot. The architects and planners made all the right choices. I'm sure I'll enjoy it.

But if I appear to be holding back my affections until it's a little weathered, a little ratty, until it gets a little dusty and until it starts to feel like part of the city's history—until, worn around the edges, it starts to feel like family—I hope you'll understand.

Orange

BUT OF COURSE it's not just brown; there is orange, too. Orange is the color of their helmets. From our seats high up in the closed end of the stadium, those helmets seem tiny, like little round bubbles when they foam up into the dugout for the player introductions at the beginning of the game, just when the crowd is reaching its peak of nervous energy. When the people filling Cleveland Municipal Stadium see those little orange circles jumble into the dugout, a roar builds from their feet, from the very concrete floor and steel girders of the stadium, to become the kind of primordial vibration I have never found anywhere else. The first glimpse of these orange bubbles whips the crowd at Cleveland Stadium into a frenzy greater than the response to any score in any game I have ever attended. They roar at the sight of those bubbles, at the sight of their beloved. They roar at the orange.

Orange is also the color of the glowing coils in the Infra-Ray heating elements that hang on bare chains above the escalators to the second deck. These provide a series of sudden, surprising warm spots on the way into the stadium as we make the trip to our seats for late-season games, while the gray stadium halls echo and boom around us and the brown-coated mass around me mumbles and steams. The expectancy of those escalator trips, with their ritual conversations between my uncle and my dad—"Can they get by these guys?" "You just gotta hope they play smart"—is almost impossibly rich, exquisite to the point of delirium.

And orange, like brown, is the color of autumn, of vibrant leaves, of pumpkins, of the giant round sun that goes down on fall Sundays when my dad watches a West Coast game in the den while my brother and I fling each other around in our tiny triangle of back lawn, playing our own one-on-one version of football. Each length of the yard is a first down, and if I am outrunning him when I get to the end of the yard we both have to freeze, then walk backwards until he hits the wall of the house, then we start running again, over and over until we've covered the distance to the mythical goal line. The house set into a hill, the family-room window comes out at about grass level, and we peer down into the room where my dad sits, drinking one of his very occasional beers. When the orange sun finally disappears, we come inside and watch the end of the first half of whatever game he's watching, then it's time for dinner. If it's an important game out on the West Coast—or the Browns are out there—we watch the whole game, and during halftime we set up the folding card table and we have dinner in there in front of the game. Afterwards, during the second half, during October and November when it's in the stores, my mom brings us bowls of candy corn. That's orange too.

Things My Father Saw

 MY DAD WAS there from the beginning.

In a way, he was there long before that. He still remembers the Cleveland Rams, who left town in 1945 perhaps because of the team Paul Brown was building. Cleveland wasn't doing much to support the Rams, and football hadn't been much of a big-time sport before then.

But those new guys—the Browns, named for that new coach of theirs, already famous for coaching Ohio State and Massillon High—quickly caught everybody's attention. "I think Paul Brown had a lot to do with it," my dad tells me. "Because he had a class team." Brown from the first told his players to behave as though they were the class act of their league. They did, and the tactic worked. "His players wouldn't go into the end zone and do a dance," my dad tells me. "You just knew he knew what he was doing with football." More than sixty thousand curiosity seekers came to the stadium for the new team's first-ever All-America Football Conference game, but my father can't claim to have been there. Still, he can recite the litany of Brown's innovations—the radio in the quarterbacks' helmets, the playbooks, the taxi squad—same as most any Browns fan. But what he remembers most is the face mask.

My dad was at the game the day Paul Brown invented the face mask because Otto Graham got bashed in the face in the first half. In the second half Graham came out with a plastic shield over his face, protecting the wound. My dad was there. My dad saw that. Perhaps captured by the team's overwhelming early success, perhaps lured by the ease of rooting for a winner, my dad found himself a Browns fan early on.

"In those days you would buy a general admission–type seat for a buck, maybe two bucks, and by the middle of the first quarter you'd be sitting on the 50-yard line," he tells me. Some people say that the Browns didn't always fill the stadium in those early days because they were simply too good—they were so certain to win that what was the point? Some say, in fact, that the Browns' success killed the AAFC, since nobody could beat them.

But my dad was one of the ones who knew, who started going early on. What was that like? What was it like to be in on the ground floor, to be one of the first seeing something that turned out to be the cultural phenomenon we call the Cleveland Browns? In those early days, with thirty, forty thousand fans, did he look into the future and see Jim Brown, Paul Warfield, Mike Phipps, the Kardiac Kids, Red Right 88, the Drive, the Fumble?

Naah. But he saw Otto Graham. My dad is not the most eloquent guy in the entire world, and he's not a guy to go on and on. But he can tell you what he saw, just in a word or two. "It was both ways," he says. "It wasn't just us loving the team. It was the team respecting us, too."

Or he'll tell you about the players. "Graham," he says. "'Automatic Otto' Graham, he'd just stand back there and nickel and dime you to death. He was smart. And he had a beautiful pass." He saw Otto Graham run plays and win games, run seasons and win championships. He remembers the disappointment of Paul Brown's lone losing season, the 5–7 in 1956—but he knows that everything turned out all right. That one bad season gave Paul Brown a high draft pick, and that turned out to be Jim Brown, and that meant another decade of excellence.

My dad watched Jim Brown run. "You would see Jim Brown run into the line, get swallowed up, and then there'd be Jim Brown, running out the other side of the line. And then he'd get tackled, and he'd get up real slow, and he'd walk real slow back to the huddle, and then they'd hand him the ball, and then off he'd go, like he never got hit in the first place. He did that every play."

Nothing eloquent about that. Nothing you don't hear from a million guys who went to Browns games in the fifties and sixties, nothing you didn't hear, probably, from your very own dad in probably exactly the same words. But your dad told you just like my dad told me, and that started something.

Because my dad talks to me about the Cleveland Browns, I know that the only year besides his rookie season that Jim Brown did *not* rush for more than a thousand yards, he was already past the thousand-yard mark before he was thrown for a five-yard loss on his final carry of the season, and ended up with 996 yards.

Because my dad talks to me about the Cleveland Browns, I know that Ernie Davis, another great Syracuse running back, came to the team in 1961 and, diagnosed with leukemia, never played a down. "I remember they introduced Ernie Davis," he recalls of the first game that fall, one of the doubleheader exhibition games, at which Davis was introduced to the fans in his street clothes. "And the place just stood and cheered, just roared. You got chills, knowing he was never going to play but he was part of the Browns.

"Would that have been something?" he asks, still remembering. "That would have been a backfield. That would have been like Brown and Kelly."

Kelly? Kelly *I* saw. By the time Leroy Kelly was nearing the end of his career, my dad was dragging me to Browns games; before I was old enough to understand the game I was occupying myself by watching the tuba players in the band get ready for halftime. But then something would happen and my dad would tell me: "That guy runs like Dante Lavelli," or "Marion Motley used to do that." My dad had history, and he shared it with me. You can say what you want about sports changing—and I certainly hope they are, and that they are becoming more inclusive and less gender specific and all of that—but in the 1960s in Cleveland, Ohio, if you learned about sports you only had one source and that was your dad.

From my dad I learned how to root for the Cleveland Browns.

There were lots of things my father told me to do that he didn't do—homework, listen to my mother, the list goes on. But loving the Browns was the opposite: something he never told me to do, something he merely did. Psychologists tell parents that it's not what they tell their kids that counts, it's what the kids see them do, and I'm living testimony. My dad didn't have to say the Browns were important—my dad *lived* the Browns being important.

And so I learned how to be a Browns fan. From that first game together against the Cowboys in 1970, my dad demonstrated his own informal code by his behavior at a Browns game. He never told me a rule about how you rooted for the Browns, but by watching him for all these years, by watching with him for all these years, I can give you an approximation of that code:

1. You cheer the Cleveland Browns, from the moment their helmets bubble up into the dugout until the moment they leave the field. You are here to support them; do so.

2. Inclement weather is part of the deal—it's part of the

fun. Rooting for the Browns when it's 10 degrees and snowing is harder than rooting for the Browns in front of your television; anybody could do that. That's what makes this fun. That's why we're here.

3. You do not cheer the Browns in a way calculated to annoy those around you, even if those around you come from different cities. First, it's impolite. Second, it can get you thrown off the second deck of the stadium.

4. When something wonderful happens, let go. You may shriek if necessary. That's why you're here—if you were truly getting all the shrieks you wanted out of life, you probably wouldn't be at a sporting event, especially one outdoors in 10-degree weather.

5. At key moments, take out a flask and have a sip of what you may politely call "tea." You don't have to wait for a victory or even a score—life isn't like that, and football needn't be either. Sometimes the small celebrations are all you're going to get that day, so enjoy them while you can.

6. Don't have too many small celebrations. You waste them that way, plus you might get drunk. Plus you might run out, and you want some left if they win.

7. Exhort the Browns to greatness however you like, especially in a way that gives clues to your own personal conflicts. For example, if your personality is such that you can rigidly deny your own anger to your own detriment, you may scream "Get mad, Browns!" every Sunday for every week of your life. When this irony is pointed out to you, you may thank God for pro football, you may sheepishly grin. You may not stop rooting for the Browns.

8. You may boo the other team when it is introduced, by way of good-natured welcome to Cleveland. You may boo extra loudly for an especially good player on the other team: "We who are about to die salute you."

9. Otherwise booing is harsh punishment and is meted out only under duress. Yet certain situations may require booing.

10. You may boo flagrantly bad officiating.

11. You may boo vicious play—in fact, you must boo vicious play.

12. Never boo genuine mistakes.

13. You may, in frustration, boo tepid play-calling and bad judgment by the coaching staff. Be prepared to justify your decision.

14. Loudly appreciate longstanding service to the team even if it's not turning out for the best—if it's Blanton Collier's final game, stand up late in the fourth quarter and cheer your lungs out even though the team is getting spanked.

15. You may boo the ownership, if you can think of a way to do it.

16. Do not boo the Cleveland Browns.

I don't think my dad could articulate this code, and if he did it might differ here and there. But after 30 years of watching my dad root for the Cleveland Browns, I can tell you that this is an accurate summation of his Browns Code. You may claim that rooting for sports teams is turning young people away from religion and country and ancestor worship or whatever else you deem more important, but I say this:

My dad told me about Jim Brown like it meant something. My dad told me about Blanton Collier like it meant something. My dad told me about Otto Graham like it meant something. He told me their history like their history was important. My dad treated the Browns like they meant something.

And you know what?

That's why they mean something.

"We always traveled first class"

A Moment with Lou Groza

LOU GROZA was the last of the old ones—the last of the original Browns still playing, a guy whose name I heard around the house in the commonplace voice used for an active player—he played until 1967—instead of in the hushed tones reserved for Graham, for Motley, for Brown. At the very beginning of my awareness, he was nothing more than the Browns' kicker, and I was surprised to learn he had been a lineman before that.

And it turns out that he's a lot more than just that. For one thing, his name comes up more than any other when former Browns players talk about their history. Maybe it's because nobody feels much of a need to mention Jim Brown or Paul Brown; maybe it's because nobody played more years for the Cleveland Browns; maybe people just like to say "The Toe" whenever they get the chance.

But maybe it's something more. Lou Groza is a man of few words from an era when that was the way men were supposed to be, an era when Paul Brown's demand that the players be personable to their fans, that they stand for something, could have raised hackles.

"He gave us the same type of training rules you'd have as a

bunch of college kids," Groza recalls from his Cleveland-area insurance office. "No drinking, no smoking . . ." The point wasn't so much that an after-practice beer or a cigarette to relax was going to wreck a player's health or destroy his performance. This was about something else. "You had to project an image," he says. "A certain kind of public image. You had to express good citizenship. You'd use the expression 'clean livers.' Guys had to hold themselves out as good examples for young kids."

But this was about even more than being a nice guy and a good ambassador for the team. This was about acting like a Cleveland Brown. "You carried a winning attitude, and you were proud of it," Groza says. Paul Brown was building an organization he said would be the New York Yankees of pro football, and everything about the organization had to demonstrate that. "And that's the thing," Groza says. "When we traveled, we always traveled first class.

"He used to use the expression he didn't want us to look like butch football players—not like the tough guy kind of guy." They wore ties, they weren't supposed to drink or smoke. Groza hesitates. "Well, he'd bend a little bit on the smoking. If you had to smoke, you smoked in your own room."

Straightforward enough for guys like Groza, who had played in a grand total of three freshman games at Ohio State before going into the service and ending up with the Browns after the war. But Brown instilled such belief in the organization he was building that even rough-living veterans who came into his organization recognized they had to fit in with the program. "The older guys, who had played professionally before the war, even they usually adhered to the rules," Groza says. "Because we had a winning attitude and were a winning group. All the years I played, of course, when Paul Brown was here, only one year did he have a losing season."

That record of success kept players focused, as did Brown's steely demeanor. "When we'd lose and look at movies of games, it wasn't a happy situation," Groza says. "He never really got close to anybody from a personality standpoint. He could call the shots on anybody without having a camaraderie situation."

The Brown magic worked on more than just the players. "The season ticket sales improved all the time," Groza recalls. "If you were having a bad year, people still would want their season tickets because they knew it wouldn't stay that way."

And Groza points out that Brown was creating more than a great organization. "Before the war, pro football really wasn't much of a sport," he says. With all of Brown's innovations— the playbook, game films, the taxi squad, the face mask, the crisp organizational regimen—Groza says that Brown was, in a way, inventing modern pro football. "After the war, it seemed like it just kept building on what he was doing."

Groza knew he was involved in something special from the Browns' very first game in the All-America Football Conference, when more than sixty thousand people watched the Browns introduced to host the Miami Seahawks. "I remember that first game in Cleveland Stadium," he says. "I'd never been there before, and it was an immense crowd. Just that alone gave you inspiration."

Groza played for fourteen years, then retired in 1960. In 1961 Paul Brown convinced him to come out of retirement to kick for the Browns again, and he played until 1967, when he retired for good. But the Browns, he says, aren't something that you stop being a part of. It's not like that at all—once you're part of the Browns, they're part of who you are forever. You may not actively participate in what they do, but they always matter.

"It's like a relative," he says. "You don't forget him. You may get some distance between you but you don't forget him.

"I'm not really an active participant," Lou Groza says. "But they're still my team."

1964

THE FIRST NAMES I remember as a child being able to pluck out of the cultural background, to recognize as significant, are John F. Kennedy, the Beatles, and Jim Brown. I can remember, during a taped replay of a Kennedy speech on television after his assassination, asking my mother how he could be talking if he were dead. So I must be old enough to remember the 1964 championship, old enough to remember my Dad and my uncle coming home chilled and elated from the stadium that day after watching the game from the bleachers, but somehow I draw a blank there. Still, I know that when the name Jim Brown is mentioned in our house, the air is electrified, a beat passes: something important has been said.

Jim Brown, as I perceive before I am old enough to understand it, is different from the rest of us. He is not just a great athlete, a beloved sports hero. He is not just the best at what he does. He is, simply, another order of being—a person one does not aspire to be like. He is a god. Nobody says so, but it's plain to see. No other topic makes my dad use the reverential tones he uses when he utters that name. I can say "Jim Brown" long before I understand what football is, or what the Browns are, or how important they are.

From long before I can understand them, the Browns are there, and they are important.

Something else is significant: winning a championship. I don't know why it's important—it certainly doesn't get you a raise at your job or cure disease or fight poverty and hate. In fact, if you look at what happens to a lot of cities the day they win championships, it doesn't look like such a victory at all.

Still: you want to win a championship. You must win a championship. It's something you have wanted since you were very small, since you were first old enough to under-stand identification with someone else, old enough to root for something. You first pick it up from your dad, probably, and then you get it in your organized sports games as a kid, then your school teams, and then in college. It won't solve your problems; it won't fix anything. But you always wish for the success of your beloved, and part of rooting for the Browns is wanting that championship. That's what it's all about.

I grew up not knowing a champion. Coming from Cleve-land, born when I was, I have never known a championship. So, like everyone else, I look back to the last one.

My dad saw the 1964 championship game. He saw it from what people used to call the bleachers and then called the Dawg Pound and now call a fond memory.

"And we froze," my dad says when I ask him to talk about it now.

That's not what he had planned. Tickets went on sale af-ter the Browns defeated the Giants in a playoff game. "The day tickets went on sale I was downtown and mailed my seat applications in from the post office downtown," he tells me. This was an effort to improve their chances, his and my uncle Sam's, of getting good seats. Seats they got; good seats they did not. They sat in the bleachers. "We watched that whole game and we just froze."

A couple years ago my dad sent every member of our family a copy of Terry Pluto's *When All the World Was Browns Town*, about that remarkable 1964 season. In it I learned about the team's struggles against the Cardinals, the quarterback rivalry between Ninowski and Ryan; about Blanton Collier's avuncular coaching, Jim Brown's stoic leadership, Art Modell's youthful energy—boding what it would. Pluto's book, a great book, filled in the details.

And I love the details—I love knowing more about what that was like. But still, for all the book's storehouse of facts, it's my dad's story that will always be mine for 1964.

Not long on details, my dad. The Browns were expected to lose and lose big. But the defense stepped up, Gary Collins caught a bunch of touchdown passes, and the Browns won 27–0, their last championship, a day remembered when I was growing up as the last moment of true greatness for the city of Cleveland. That's about it. The Browns were supposed to lose, the Browns won, it was very cold. The thing is, of course, that's enough. It's enough because it's what he can tell me. I'll always yearn for my own champion to cheer, but until then I know he had his, and that he went out there to cheer them.

Just knowing he was there is enough.

"It can't be just a bunch of guys in brown uniforms"

A Moment with Jim Brown

THE NAME STILL SOUNDS as powerful as it did more than 30 years ago, and just saying it still creates a thrill:

Jim Brown.

It's like saying "Babe Ruth," like saying "General Motors," like saying "the Empire State Building."

It's saying, "football player"—his name defines the term. In other sports you can argue about who was the greatest ever—Ruth, Cobb, Aaron, Mays; Russell, Havlicek, Jordan, Jabbar. You can make a case for a lot of guys. Not football. It's a given: Jim Brown was the greatest football player ever, and it's going to be a long time before anybody dominates the game the way he did. It's not an argument: It's a fact, and fans of the Browns are no more aware of it than fans of other teams.

But he did play for the Browns. The NFL was born in northeastern Ohio, in Canton; Paul Brown invented the modern game in Massillon, in Columbus, and in Cleveland. So somehow, Jim Brown had to end up in Cleveland, with the Browns. It's even been suggested half seriously that Paul Brown engineered his only losing season the year that it enabled him to draft Jim Brown. The implication is absurd, of course, but there does seem to be a destiny at work, a kind of necessity.

And yet Jim Brown didn't get it at first.

"I didn't know at the time" what playing for the Browns would be like, he said from the Los Angeles office of his Amer-I-Can organization. "I thought I wanted to go to New York, because I had history in New York"—he had gone to high school on Long Island and college at Syracuse. "I knew the Browns had been successful, with Graham and Willis and Motley, but not until I got there did I really know what it was like.

"What really surprised me was the intensity of the fans— the honesty of the fans, and the enduring kind of memory that the fans had." Even when he went on a book tour years after he retired, Brown says that Browns fans demonstrated something very different from the kind of simple hero worship he might have expected. "Before that, I thought it had just been a matter of football," he said. "But it was more than that. It was relationships and memories, between fathers and sons, and mothers and daughters. Families had gone to those games and had related in beautiful ways and would always remember and identify with me, with the Browns.

"I did not know it ran that deep."

But oh, boy, does it. And Brown has come to cherish that connection, that sincere appreciation. "What I have found most impressive is [how the fans acted] after I left football," he says. He figures you can expect people to appreciate you when you're playing for their team. But when you've been gone for decades, when you've been replaced by other heroes dozens of times but they still appreciate and respect you, "that's when I had a chance to see how they really felt," Brown says. "They have other stars, but they kept giving that love and respect. That's a good friend. That's a really good friend. That means they still respect you. That means they're thinking people and feeling people. Which is a good combination."

Thinking people and feeling people. A nice thing to say about Browns fans, and Brown knows it. Part of that special relationship came from Paul Brown, from the players, Jim Brown knows—but an awful lot of it starts with the fans and with the city.

"I think it's part of the tradition of Ohio," he says. "Massillon, football, part of the people. It's just the way you view football in Ohio. They say Browns fans are like blue-collar people, regular people."

He thinks for a moment about how to explain how Browns fans are a little different than others. Like Packers fans, he explains, they seem to have held on to the values of a previous era of fandom. Even today, Browns fans are still a little more like the fans he played for, the fans Otto Graham played for. "I guess it's like playing in the sixties versus playing in the nineties," he says. "You have a great game now, a lot of flash, a lot of stardom, but the heart . . . a lot of heart has gone out of the game because of money."

Heart is what it was about for Jim Brown, playing for Paul Brown, playing for the Browns. He remembered that year where his thousand-yard season was lost because the game just wasn't over yet, and his final carry set him back short of the mark. "That's absolutely right. Certain things would have been unheard of—one of them is to deliberately prepare for a record. The record had to come in the course of a game. That was part of the Cleveland tradition—that was Paul Brown. You'd never walk up to Paul Brown and talk about breaking a record. It gets a little funny when you start setting things up for reasons other than winning the ball game or finishing the ball game."

But that heart has never left Cleveland, at least not among

the fans. "I have a 1969 Mercedes," Brown says. "It's a classic. The way they were built, it's just classic. And I have a 1998 Mustang. The Mustang is fast and quick and got all kinds of stereo equipment, but the quality is not close to the workmanship of my Mercedes.

"So Cleveland would be like a classic Mercedes. History and workmanship and details, so the fans are that way." It's that history, that tradition, that solidity that Brown admires. That's why, for example, when the final game rolled around in 1995, Brown went out and sat in the Dawg Pound. "I said, 'Well, when it's over it's over, so I might as well be out here with you guys.'"

And about that franchise move, Brown makes the same choice. "I'm connected with the fans—with the city, and the state. And I can do that without ever defending anyone else, without ever losing the purity of it. Ownership will change, but the history and the sharing that I've had with the fans and the game belongs to me and is precious to me. No one can say I'm not a Brown and don't respect and care about the Browns. Those fans will always be precious to me and that history will be precious to me."

Another thing precious to Brown is that 1964 championship. "That's always the goal," he says. "You have so many members on a team, with different jobs. And the only time it all comes together is when you become the number one team. That became the highlight of my career, because it was such a team victory.

"Everybody contributed. That made it a happy occasion for everybody. To have the defense contribute, the way they played—that lives forever in the world of sports."

Asked whether he was still a fan of the Browns, Jim Brown responded in a way befitting the best player in the game's history. "I'm a fan of great play. I'm a fan of dedication and a lot of heart. I do pull for the Browns, and I pull for them dearly. But I recognize good play wherever it comes from. I don't want the game to be just a matter of who wins it. I want you guys to execute well, I want you to play hard, and if you do that and lose then I'm with you. But lousy football, careless football, if you're out of shape, then I'm not with that. It can't be just a bunch of guys in brown uniforms who go out on the field."

As for Jim Brown's most memorable moment, that too comes right down to the fans, and to heart. It wasn't that 1964 championship game. It wasn't running for 237 yards in a game twice. It wasn't the MVP awards or the records.

"The moment I remember most, I wasn't playing anymore, and David Modell invited me back. He reached out and asked me to come back and let him introduce me. I don't know if Art really knew how the fans were going to accept me, and he wasn't sure about this."

But Brown came back.

"When I was introduced, I got a three, four, five minute standing ovation." Brown gives a contented sigh. "I didn't know what they were going to do. But they gave it up. That remains in my mind as a fantastic moment between the Cleveland Browns and myself.

"I don't remember what day it was," Jim Brown says. "But I've got a picture."

So, to be sure, do we all.

The Cincinnati Game

THE WEST THIRD STREET BRIDGE is the holy road, the Via Sacra of the initiates in Brown, and the first regret I have concerning the Cleveland Browns is that my father, my uncle, and I never had our pictures taken by the guy who stood on that bridge with what looked to be a modified eight-millimeter movie camera, snapping photos of people in the crowd as they streamed by on their way to the stadium. If he caught you he'd hand you a white slip of paper with a number on it, which apparently corresponded to a frame in his spool of film, and if you sent him some money he would develop that frame and send you a grainy, fuzzy, snapshot of you and your party looking the wrong way as you walked by him.

"Your mom and I sent for one once," my dad said, "and you could barely even tell it was us," so we knew not to fall for such foolishness a second time. But by standing on the West Third Street Bridge in that river of humanity the picture man demonstrated that this was something special, the type of event for which you might conceivably want a record of your attendance. I had been to Indians games, to the art museum, to Disney World, and to New York City, to high holiday services and to funerals, and at none of those did anyone commemorate your presence on film—they left the photography to whoever wanted it. Only at weddings did someone take a picture of everyone showing up, did someone treat your just being there as inherently worthy of celebration. Only at weddings, that is, and Browns games.

But I scarcely needed the picture man to teach me that

these games, these gatherings of eighty thousand to roar together, were important. Everything about my father's preparation for the games, everything about his Sunday morning rituals—reading the sports, poring over the lineups—said the Browns were important. Or no, not important, worth it: he got so much joy from them that the Browns were, for whatever reasons, worthy of love and support.

So I went with him, part of something my dad, my uncles, my brother shared, though at first I did not understand. I went to these games, and I raked the crowd with my binoculars, I watched the marching bands prepare for the halftime show, I watched the little swing band in the photographers' dugout pep up the crowd during television time-outs. The electricity of the game affected me, but still, somehow, perhaps too young at 12 years old, perhaps merely too dreamy and passive, I hadn't been caught. Perhaps I hadn't absorbed enough to really understand what I was seeing. Perhaps I had just never seen a great game.

And then, in early December 1971, my dad took me to the Cincinnati game. Cincinnati was my dad's second-favorite team. "They're Paul Brown's team," he said, "and Paul Brown started the Browns." End of explanation.

But as we bundled out the door that gray November day after Sam honked the horn down in front of the house, my dad said something else. "But I think I'm going to like them a little bit less by the end of the day." The Browns were 6–5, showing a little life; Pittsburgh wasn't as good as everyone had expected, and with three games to go, the Browns suddenly had a chance to make a move for a playoff spot. The Bengals, though, had won the division the year before, with Paul Brown for the second time in his life shepherding a new team from a suspect league into instant credibility in the newly merged NFL. It looked to be the Bengals' day, at least to my dad.

I number my days as a true Browns fan from the events of that afternoon. Perhaps those early games had prepared me, or I had finally heard enough football talk to start, somehow, to get it—but that day when we parked our car in our little alley parking lot downtown, as the trickle from the parking lot joined a stream down towards Public Square, poured into the rush of men disgorged from the Terminal and became part of the river flowing to the West Third Street Bridge, I felt something more than just a child's fascination with the colors, the bustle, of a crowd. As my dad and Sam talked about the game, I held onto the belt of my dad's gray felt jacket not just so that I didn't lose him, but because I didn't want to miss the conversation. I felt, for the first time, part of all this, and when my father crumpled and discarded the numbered slip from the picture man I remember wishing that this one time we could have bought the picture.

My uncle Sam, for reasons I've never understood, began explaining to me why you almost never leave a game early. "Unless it's a total laugher one way or the other," he said, "you stick around. Why not? You paid for the ticket." My dad recalled the time, with the Browns entering the fourth quarter of a bad-weather game down three touchdowns to the Giants, they had decided to beat the traffic and leave the game—and listened on the radio to the Browns score four times in the fourth quarter and win.

Inside the stadium, I noticed for the first time the rising tension in the atmosphere. I felt the conversation die around me, until the music, the Browns song, playing over the public address system, began bouncing a little more freely among the girders and latticework. The people hadn't stopped talking so much as changed their tone, from the light babbling of easy conversation to the strained mutters and murmurs of impatience—"Come on, come on," men said. "All right, let's go."

Here and there gloved hands clapped, booted feet shuffled and stamped, and the clock hands inched their way towards one o'clock. The rectangular pale green field stopped looking like a meadow, like a lawn. The players, finished warming up, had left it, and with the lights turned on against the leaden, overcast sky, the field seemed stark and lonely.

Then, from across the stadium, a swelling of noise. It started around the 50-yard line of the west side of the stadium, and bit by bit it worked its way around the horseshoe until it enveloped us. I stood up with my dad and uncle and watched the two of them clap, watched their faces radiate a kind of fierce, directed joy, mirrored on the faces of the men around them. I saw but did not understand, until my uncle saw my confusion and pointed—there, down on the field, coming out of the tunnel, were those orange helmets, bubbling into the dugout. "There they are, buddy!" Sam said. "Look! It's the Browns!"

And there they were. "They look ready!" my dad shouted, and they truly did—something about the way the players juked and hopped, the way they bobbed and shuffled together, looked strong. I did not know it then, but I would become a connoisseur of this first-moment tea-leaf reading.

Then the announcer introduced the Bengals, and the crowd booed in a good-natured way. Then, after a pause, he introduced the Browns' offense, leaving running back Leroy Kelly for last, and when Kelly ran onto the field—"and the rest of the Cleveland Browns!"—the moment was over. My dad pulled out his flask, and he and Sam had a sip, and it was time to get going.

I wasn't caught yet, but by God I was interested. When the Bengals fumbled the opening kickoff I cheered, genuinely cheered, for the first time understanding what I was seeing. The Browns quickly scored, and, showing off my newfound knowledge, I confidently turned to my uncle Sam: "So it looks like it's going to be a laugher, huh."

He shrugged. "A lot of football left to play," he said. "Let's just see what happens." On cold days he wore under his coat a sweatshirt, and with its pointed hood atop his head balanced by the pointed beard poking down from his chin, he looked a little like an elf—the brownie logo that the Browns sometimes used always reminded me of him. The Browns kicked off again, and I cared what happened. I was becoming part of it.

It wasn't a laugher, or not for the Browns, anyway. The Bengals recovered from their first-play gaffe and started to play football, whereas the Browns never got much going after that early gift touchdown. Before the second quarter was half over the Bengals led 20–7. The Browns scored a touchdown late in the first half, though, and despite being badly outplayed were down by only six at the half.

During halftime, after the marching bands finished but before we had finished the coffee and pastrami sandwiches we had brought from home, the Browns had a little ceremony at the 50-yard line honoring Dr. Vic Ippolito, retiring as team physician after decades of service. And if I was too young to appreciate the Browns publicly honoring people like team physicians, I was also too young to effortlessly tune out the platitudes, and so I was paying close attention when Ippolito opened his brief remarks by saying, "Stick around, because we're going to win this one." A thrill touched me then, and as the stadium gave a game, weakly optimistic cheer, I felt the first tickle of something like belief.

As the second half began I was practicing the use of binoculars, teaching myself when to focus on the quarterback, when to watch the linemen, and when to drop them and watch the whole field. So it was pure luck that I was watching wide receiver Frank Pitts as he ran a fly pattern up the right sideline, underneath a floater from quarterback Bill Nelson, and saw two Cincinnati defenders leap up in front of Pitts as the ball came down—and knock one another away, the ball somehow finding its way into the hands of Pitts, who glided into the end zone as the entire stadium stood to roar. My dad and Sam leapt to their feet, jumping up and down and slapping one another on the back, but I just sat down, dropping my binoculars into my lap and repeating to myself: "He caught it! He caught it!" and starting to cry. It was the most beautiful thing I had ever seen.

The Bengals came back for another couple of field goals, and the Browns answered with one of their own. As the fourth quarter ticked by, the Browns, down 27–24, started a drive towards us, into the closed end of the stadium. A cheer, unrelated to anything on the field, filled the place, and I looked around. My dad pointed to the scoreboard, which showed that the lowly Houston Oilers had just put up another score on the Steelers, who now were certain to lose. "That means if the Browns win this game," my dad told me, "they clinch the division. They're in the playoffs if they win."

I don't remember much about the drive except that it was the most important thing that had ever happened in the entire history of the world. I do remember that shortly before the two-minute warning Leroy Kelly ran around left end, met a Bengals linebacker, and leapt as high as he could, swinging the ball over the goal line and putting the Browns up 31–27. My dad, my uncle, and I performed a kind of mad dance I had never before seen, much less participated in. My uncle, in his elfin hood, jumped up and down so high that I feared he would tumble down over the outstretched arms of the fans below us and fall off the upper deck. He didn't, though, and he and my dad had some tea from my dad's flask, and so did I.

The Bengals had the ball for a last chance, but with a field goal of no use to them, they started throwing the ball downfield, where an interception by Ernie Kellermann ended the suspense quickly. The Browns ran out the clock, and as my dad, my uncle, and eighty thousand other people chanted down the final seconds, I watched the Browns make their way into the playoffs. For most of the people there, it was another great Browns win leading to another playoff game and maybe even another championship. For me it was more than the first great win I ever saw. It was a change in the world: I cared about the Cleveland Browns.

Filing along the concrete halls in a sea of brown and orange we didn't talk, but the excited babble as we circled the stadium concourse sounded like music, it sounded like everything that was ever perfect to a 12-year-old boy. As we emerged from the shadows of the stadium I again held my dad's belt, and as we dodged the crowd going back over the bridge, together we were Leroy Kelly, and we were scoring a touchdown and going into the playoffs, all of us, together.

We got to our car and drove home, listening on the radio to Gib Shanley scold the fans who were then pulling down the goalposts, and my dad and my uncle laughed as we rode. Among the brown buildings and gray streets, fog billowed into the cold air through the manhole covers.

Brown on Brown

A Moment with Mike Brown

MIKE BROWN dismisses the similarities immediately. "Oh, there really wasn't any connection," he says of the Bengals' black-and-orange uniforms, their initials, the fact that in every way they seemed to be a copy of the Browns. "There was a football team in Cincinnati in the old days named the Bengals, and they just used the same name," says Brown, who's now the president and general manager of the second football team his father, Paul Brown, started. "The other reason was it had a tiger motif, like Massillon High School [where Paul Brown used to coach]. Once you choose Bengal tigers you're orange and black. Early on the uniforms did look very similar, and Art complained about that." Modell lobbied hard for a change in the Bengals' uniforms, and the Bengals ended up with their current tiger stripes. "My dad's comment on that was, who was changing whose uniform? Anyway, that Browns uniform was emulated or adopted all over. Green Bay's uniform was just the Browns uniform, except it was yellow and green."

Okay, Mike, it's all one vast coincidence—Paul Brown didn't care one way or the other whether his Bengals were playing the Cleveland Browns or the Buffalo Bills. It was all the same to Paul Brown whether he was going up against just some other football team or the team that he had invented, led to championships, turned into the greatest organization in football—the team that bore his name. The team that, when his productivity flagged, when a few seasons went by without a champion, pushed him out the door.

Brown backs off a little. "Well, there was a good rivalry between Cincinnati and the Browns, and he'd look forward to that. Those early games, they were important to us, to my father, to me. Cleveland was our big rival, and it was keenly felt by everyone down here. My dad had some feeling about those games. I think Art did as well."

But when you talk to Mike Brown about Paul Brown he doesn't really want to get into those hard feelings—in fact, he says that though the rivalry was there, and there was no game Paul Brown wanted the Bengals to win like a game against the Browns, in all other ways, his dad loved the Browns until the day he died. "They still had a place in my dad's heart—and not a small place, either. He never left that behind. That was always with him. He wanted to beat the Browns where we were playing them, but he never lost his love for the guys who had been with him or the city or all that went with it."

In fact, it's those guys that Paul Brown chose for his team that made the Browns the best organization in football, Mike says. When describing the connection between town and team, that special bond of Brown, he points to the Browns breaking the color barrier without any fuss, his father hiring players like Marion Motley before Jackie Robinson began playing major league baseball. His dad wasn't trying to make a point, Mike says: "He knew these guys. He knew they were great players and he invited them in very simply because he knew they were better than the players we had. He paid very little heed to a code [of segregation] that then existed because it was not his code."

And Browns' fans connected with that. "That reflected the viewpoint of northern Ohio," Mike says. "They were not bigoted. The views were [those] of my dad and his community, which was northern Ohio, and it brought that community together. No one thought much about it, at least in Cleveland. It was just accepted."

It was just accepted. Maybe that's part of the bond—a northeastern Ohio coach starts a northeastern Ohio team with players from northeastern Ohio (Paul Brown knew Marion Motley, for example, because when Brown coached Massillon, Motley played for Canton McKinley; he also showed special attention to guys who played for Ohio State). Naturally enough, everybody kind of shares the same values. Northeastern Ohio is a progressive place, so nobody pays much mind when some of the ballplayers on their team turn out to be black, and suddenly there's another bond between players and fans. Another way the Cleveland Browns start to stand for something. They have a standard of decency, of self-respect.

"We had standards of conduct that he thought were . . . proper," Mike says. "Higher. The thing that was good about that was that the players responded for the most part positively. Guys were proud to be part of the Browns. Proud that their peers were high-grade, classy. They liked being identified with that standard. They knew they could count on each other. They knew that guys would not embarrass the team or them. That aura surrounded the team." His dad drafted as much for the ability to fit into that culture of respect as for football skills. It worked.

And now the Brown legacy has two strains—one in Cleveland, one in Cincinnati. And as the rivalry starts again, so will those tiny stirrings of support from one town to another. "He had a lot of friends in Cleveland," Mike Brown says of his father's later days. "A lot of those old players were a big part of his life until the day he died. He didn't walk away from any of that."

And now there's a new batch of guys who'll become those old players, and like sons of Browns fans carrying on their dads' legacy of caring, Mike Brown will carry on his father's legacy of respect and good will. "Yeah, there will always be great pride in all that happened with the old Browns," he says. "Cleveland is where I grew up. In my mind, that's my hometown. And I want them to succeed."

Mike Brown hesitates. "They have a place in my heart," he laughs.

"Except when we see 'em."

"We want Phipps!"

 I TALK TO FRIENDS—other Browns fans—about growing up Brown, and we identify ourselves by era. My dad came up in what I think of as the Elder Days—the Otto Graham years, when the Browns were doing what Paul Brown had hoped they'd do, acting like the New York Yankees of football. He grew interested, going to the occasional game, and keeping up a low-level commitment until the Jim Brown years, when he was truly hooked. I think of that as the "True Brown" era—he was rooting for a club whose coach, best player, and team were all named Brown.

Me? I grew up in the "We want Phipps" era. Which is to say, my life as a Browns fan has always been defined by something I desperately wanted but could not get—the championship those of us 40 and younger are still waiting to experience. If you want to strengthen a relationship, don't give somebody something. Until they get what they want they'll never leave, and I'm certainly still here.

When Mike Phipps showed up, it was only six years since the Browns' most recent championship. And Mike Phipps was supposed to be the answer. Mike Phipps was supposed to bring the next one.

My first memory of Mike Phipps goes back to the gymnasium of Cleveland Heights High School in early 1970, when my dad took my brother and me to see the Cleveland Browns play a charity basketball game against a bunch of teachers. I have two overwhelming memories of that day.

The first was the players' physical size. I had never seen the Browns in person before, and I was unprepared for their massiveness. Defensive lineman Jim Kanicki was at one point provoked into putting a headlock on an opponent, and I remember thinking if Kanicki flexed his bicep the guy's head might pop off like a dandelion.

I also remember the crowd—not huge, but there were plenty of guys there—clapping during the introduction of the Browns players as they trotted one by one onto the floor in shorts and gray T-shirts. And then this one wiry guy glided through the door, his legs striding but his torso moving as smoothly as if he sat on a bicycle, and the place erupted. Every fan was on his feet, cheering, applauding, screaming in an ovation that would not stop. I turned to my dad, wide-eyed. "Wow!" I asked. "Is he a great basketball player?"

My dad shook his head—"No," he said. "That's Paul Warfield."

And he had just been traded to the Miami Dolphins for a draft choice, so that the Browns could get to the third position in the draft and grab up this Purdue quarterback named Mike Phipps, and this ovation was the fans' thanks to Warfield for his six years of unforgettable service to the club, with an undercurrent of dissent, commentary on a trade of which they did not approve.

My memories of becoming truly Brown weave themselves around Mike Phipps like ivy around a tree. In those first few Browns games I attended in 1970, the team stumbled badly, partly because quarterback Bill Nelson had no Warfield to throw to. By the time I was attending my first games in 1971—Phipps was then barely more than a raw rookie—every time the Browns failed to move on a possession or two, a chant would begin, first trailing around the bleachers and the ragged edges of the upper-deck cheap seats: "We want Phipps!" the fans would shout. "We want Phipps!"

Maybe the fans were impatient to get some results from the guy for whom they had lost Warfield; maybe they were irritated at the bad showing of 1970; maybe it was just something to shout to keep warm. But "We want Phipps!" it was, every time the aging Bill Nelson failed to get a first down, and with each week it got stronger. By midway through the season—after a 27–0 blanking by the Denver Broncos, after a 31–14 drubbing by the Falcons—those chants were loud, loud, loud.

Still, as the year progressed, the Browns, aided by some late-career heroics from Leroy Kelly, rode a 9–5 record into the playoffs, yet the fans grew increasingly restive, frustrated that Bill Nelson did the quarterbacking. The chants never stopped—and, in fact, stayed in the stadium for the Indians' season the next summer, when a tiring pitcher for the Tribe would elicit chants of "We want Phipps!" from sarcastic fans.

In 1972, Phipps took his shot. With a stingy defense and the erratic but occasionally brilliant Frank Pitts as a target—and with Nelson more as coach than backup—Phipps looked like he just might be as good as the Browns hoped he was. The Browns went 10–4, with Phipps directing a two-minute drill at the end of the home game against Pittsburgh that resulted in a Don Cockroft field goal with less than 10 seconds on the clock and a 26–24 Browns win.

At that time I labored under the belief that listening to a game on the radio jinxed the Browns, so I hadn't listened, instead breathlessly watching, with my friend, as the scores from other games popped up on whatever game was televised in Cleveland that day. And when my father came to the door an hour later, his face flushed, we stopped him in the foyer and made him replay the final drive before he even got his coat off.

"It was something," he said. "That Nelson stood in there, cool as anything, throwing passes—"

"Nelson!" we cried, dismayed. "Nelson?"

My dad was as surprised as we were at the sound of the word. "Did I say Nelson? No—it was Phipps. It was Phipps! He was something." He was—on that day he was something.

But that was it—that was Phipps's day; that was his day to be Brown. The Browns made the playoffs that year but lost to the Dolphins; the *Plain Dealer* ran a big story on Phipps and his wife in which he talked about how nice the extra week's pay was. He wasn't too heated up over a single playoff game. He—and the Browns, and the fans—had more in mind. It looked like the start of something big.

But it wasn't. That was the only playoff game Mike Phipps played with the Browns. Things went downhill for the Browns after that. By the 1975 season fans sometimes chanted "We want Phipps!" only Phipps was already in the game. Maybe they were drunk, maybe they were sarcastic, maybe it was just something to chant to keep warm. But Mike Phipps did not save the Browns.

Phipps never did what Brownies hoped he'd do, and in 1976 he separated his shoulder in the first game, and Brian Sipe stepped in. At the end of that season Phipps was traded to the Bears, ending an era.

Oddly, though, "We want Phipps" lived on, echoing around the stadium when the Browns weren't getting the job done, an ironic comment from fans who thought they'd never need to get used to losing but were surprised to find that they were. In 1995, at the last Cleveland–Pittsburgh game in the old stadium—the last gasp of the old rivalry—when Vinny Testaverde was failing to produce for those dispirited short-termers waiting to move to Baltimore, I sat with my brother and sister in the closed end of the stadium and tried again: "We want Phipps," we shouted. "We want Phipps!"

People laughed, and it was wonderful, and it was wonderful not because of Mike Phipps, a fine pro ballplayer who had a couple bad breaks and now works in insurance in Fort Lauderdale. No, it was funny because we remembered, all of us there, wanting Phipps, wanting him so badly. Those were dark days in Cleveland, those early seventies days. The Hough riots were part of our lives then; the Cuyahoga River catching fire was part of our lives then. Mayor Ralph Perk's hair catching fire and the plants closing and the jobs leaving and the city declining and goddamn it, nobody was doing anything about any of it, and the Indians had been terrible since before anybody could remember, and now even the Browns—the Browns! Ten championship games in ten seasons! Jim Brown, the best football player ever!—now even the Browns were no good, and we wanted somebody to do something about it and goddamn it we wanted Phipps.

And he couldn't save us, and he couldn't save our city, and it turned out nobody could, at least not then. But what Cleveland wanted from Mike Phipps I don't know if it ever wanted more from anybody—not from Paul Brown or Jim Brown, who gave it to them, and not from Brian Sipe or Bernie Kosar, who tried so hard but couldn't.

Cleveland wanted Phipps, and when it got him, he didn't transform us, he didn't turn us back into perennial winners. We wanted Phipps and he taught us the hardest lesson. That those days when we always won—that those days when even if we had a bad series, a bad game, even a bad season, it would all be all right next year, that those days when one bad season would enable the Browns to draft Jim Brown, when the brain trust would find some seventh-rounder who would turn out to be Leroy Kelly—that those days were gone. They will never be back—we'll never catch lightning in a bottle the way Paul Brown did. Jim Brown was a once-in-a-lifetime guy; Jim Brown will never be back.

The Browns are coming back, of course. The city of Cleveland has come back and is sailing along. But in some ways—and it's for the better, if you think about it—we'll always want Phipps.

"I gave it my best"

A Moment with Mike Phipps

 MIKE PHIPPS laughs when I offer the theory that he may have stood in for a lot of unmet hopes and dreams of Clevelanders going through a difficult civic period, that he probably would have had to win the Super Bowl, clean up Lake Erie, and defeat Ralph Perk for mayor to give the Browns fans what they thought he owed them. "That's a pretty tall order," he says from his Fort Lauderdale office.

But there may be something to it, he allows. He played for the Browns for seven years, and though he didn't put pressure on himself to be the savior that the Browns—and the city—had him sketched out to be, he certainly was aware of their feelings. He knew the team had traded Paul Warfield for him, and that was a lot to give up. "At the time, I didn't know if it was going to be a big deal or not," he says. "But I think it was. I'd have to say too that not all the players probably agreed with that trade, so I didn't come in [to] open arms. There were some people I had to win over."

Half a town demands that you be a savior, and the other half wishes you'd never showed up. Not an easy role. "But that's the way it was played out," he says. "I don't know if I had extra pressure, but certainly I had some things I needed to do to kind of correct those situations."

Like, for example, listen to those "We want Phipps!" chants and just show up ready to play. "I do remember that," he says. "I guess I realized that my time was coming. I didn't know it was going to be after those chants, but it was coming." And he remembers the moments where it all seemed to be coming through. "I remember that Pittsburgh game in 1972," he says, when he ran that last-minute drive through the rain for the winning field goal. He remembers a touchdown pass here, a good call there. He remembers waiting in the tunnel to that old dugout in the stadium for player introductions, though he says he didn't experience the chills other players recall from that moment. In the first place, he says, "I was just trying to focus." In the second place, "I never really was quite certain what greeting I was going to get. There was always a mixture."

Ironically, Phipps became friends with Warfield. The two would work out together at the Browns' facility in the off-season, Warfield working on his cuts and Phipps working on his arm. "I could see what he was like, and it was like, 'Wow, wouldn't it be wonderful to have a couple of these guys running around.' It kind of became a dream of mine to throw a touchdown pass to him." But Warfield played for the Dolphins, and then in the World Football League, and Phipps was trying to lead a bunch of Browns, mostly past their prime, to a postseason that after 1972 eluded them. In 1973 they went 7–5–2, in 1974 they dropped to 4–10, in 1975 to 3–11. Greg Pruitt kept the fans excited with his tearaway jerseys and hectic scampers, Milt Morin hauled in passes over the middle, Jerry Sherk tried to stake down a weakening defense. There were great games to remember, if not seasons; and there were great plays to remember, if not games.

The play Phipps remembers above all was a play he called the Great Escape—"I think if I had to really take one play in one game that was really exciting for everyone it was the game we played Pittsburgh at home, I think in 1973. We were coming back late in the fourth quarter, and that's when they had Greenwood and White and Joe Greene and Ernie Holmes.

"I dropped back to pass and the pocket collapsed. I think four of the guys were on top of me. They thought I had gone down and somehow I slipped out of the pocket. I'm not even sure how I did it, but it was like I snuck out of the pile, and I hit Greg Pruitt down the sideline for a play that kept the drive alive.

"It was an amazing play. You couldn't see me on the films, and all of a sudden I came out of this pile."

An amazing play that sounds exactly like the way my dad describes Jim Brown: "He'd go into the line," my dad will say, "and he'd get swallowed up, and then—ploop!—out would come Jim Brown, on the other side of the line." It sounds like a great play. Except my dad doesn't remember the Great Escape. My brother doesn't remember the Great Escape. I don't remember the Great Escape. Greg Pruitt remembers it, and some other die-hard Browns fans remember it, but the Great Escape lives in the memories of only the few. Certainly those were dark years for the Browns, and Mike Phipps spent an awful lot of time running for his life, and when he got a pass off plenty of times it was because he managed some kind of Houdini act.

But still, the time Mike Phipps worked that Browns magic to its highest degree, the time he felt his own hair stand on end from the marvelousness of what he had done—that moment, that play has all but disappeared. We all remember the Drive. We all remember Red Right 88. We all remember the Fumble. But mostly, we don't remember the Great Escape.

In 1976, Warfield, freed from the World Football League, rejoined the Browns—and Phipps lived his dream, connecting with Warfield for a touchdown in the first half of the very first game. In fact, Phipps threw three touchdowns in that first half, and with Warfield and Reggie Rucker to throw to, it looked like Phipps and the Browns might be going somewhere.

Except right after halftime the only place Phipps was going was to the hospital. A separated shoulder ended that dream, and by the time he returned to the Browns in the thirteenth game they belonged to another quarterback, a guy named Brian Sipe.

That's what it was to have been anointed the savior of the Browns. That's what it was to have come to town in exchange for maybe the best wide receiver ever to play the game. Still, nobody guarantees you nothing, not in this league and not on this team. On this team you wear a suit when you travel, you smoke in your room if you smoke, you sign autographs, and you hold your head high. If you're a Brown, you act like a Brown, and you don't whine.

And when you're asked about the career that started with all those hopes and ended with a trade to the Bears, you smile loud enough for it to travel over the phone lines.

"Well," Phipps says, "I gave it my best."

That's being Brown.

"I see what Paul Brown saw"

A Moment with Paul Warfield

THE FIRST THING you need to know about Paul Warfield is that he is a little embarrassed to be mentioned in the same breath as Jim Brown, Lou Groza, Paul Brown. "For me, as a youngster, those guys were . . . like Ruth and Gehrig and Mantle and DiMaggio," Warfield says from his Miami home. "The monuments beyond center field in Yankee Stadium."

That's not the last time he mentions the Yankees in comparison with the Browns. In fact, he says that's the only comparison you can make. "There should be monuments down there in that new stadium," he says. "What Cleveland football means, the only comparable situation would be the Yankees. That was Paul Brown's objective, and I think he very much accomplished his goal in making the Browns synonymous with winning.

"I see Cleveland as being only one kind of football team— only one kind of organization. I see what Paul Brown saw. I'll always be supportive of them; that's what they represent to me."

Then there's one other thing you need to know about Paul Warfield. He's not a real emotional guy. "Pretty deadpan, as a matter of fact," he says, with a small chuckle. Usually considered low key and even emotionless on the field, he was a professional, wanting nothing more than to get the job done. That he did, of course—from 1964 to 1969 with the Browns, where he was already considered one of the best wide receivers ever to play the game, and from 1970 through 1974, with Miami, where he cemented his Hall of Fame credentials by being perhaps the most potent weapon on a team that won the Super Bowl twice. A year wasted in the World Football League left Paul Warfield master of his own destiny, a free agent—and he headed right back to Cleveland, where he played two more years before hanging 'em up.

All those thrilling wins and heartbreaking losses, the 1964 title with the Browns and titles in 1972 and 1973 with the Dolphins. All that, and Paul Warfield got emotional—felt the tears brim up—exactly twice, by his own estimation.

The second time is easy enough to guess. He sat in the stadium before his last Cleveland game, he says, knowing that for the last time ever he was going to walk out onto the field in front of screaming fans. "The walk downstairs into the bowels of the stadium, down that long dark tunnel, gradually hearing the echoes and roars of the crowd intensify as we got toward the lighted portion. Then once we came out onto the field, that roar was deafening."

Warfield laughs. "If a player could not get charged up by coming out of that tunnel, he was certifiably dead." So getting ready to walk out that tunnel for the last time brought out the deep sighs, the watery eyes. "As I was sitting and lacing up my shoulder pads and putting my jersey on, I got a little bit teary eyed. The impact of these fans and their relationship was such a great tribute to me."

The other time occurred at the stadium too, but earlier, when he was wearing an unfamiliar shade of aqua.

It was in 1973, on Monday night, when the Dolphins visited Cleveland for the first time. "It's Monday night football, and

I was a member of the opposing team, for the introduction of the starting lineups," he recalls. He'd been around for those introductions many times wearing orange and brown, and he knew: "The opponents' lineup is always met with a chorus of boos that is as deafening as the roar for the Browns," he says. But then he stood in the visitors' dugout, heard his teammates on offense being introduced, and then heard the announcer call out: "At wide receiver . . . number 42 . . . Paul Warfield!" And he ran out into the middle of the field.

And every one of the eighty thousand people in Cleveland Municipal Stadium stood and roared, pouring out the love for a player they had never gotten over losing. "When I was introduced that night I got a standing ovation," Warfield says. "When I received that introductory standing ovation from the entire sports crowd of Cleveland, my eyes were filling. I even gave a wave to the fans, an uncustomary thing for me."

So what was it about those fans, what was it about that appreciation that could coax emotion even out of a consummate professional like Warfield?

"It dispelled the myth," Warfield said—of fan fickleness, of fans being homers and front-runners, rooting for their guys, for winners and ignoring everyone else.

"It dispelled the myth: How soon do they forget. That clearly pointed out: They don't forget. They didn't forget."

That's Browns fans. They don't forget. And because the fans don't forget, the players don't forget, and that culture of belief bounces back and forth forever. As much as it lives in the stands, it lives just as strongly in the locker room. That's the pressure of history Warfield felt when he came to the Browns as a rookie, playing with Jim Brown and Lou Groza, guys who had built the Browns name.

"They were the guys who established the tradition, who won every Sunday," he says. "Those standards were lofty ones, and I wanted to fit in so badly, and contribute to that success. I'm proud of the fact that I did it, but it's still a little bit difficult for me."

He'll just have to get used to it. On a building in down-town Cleveland, to commemorate the rebirth of the Browns, there's a new mural. In the mural you see likenesses of Otto Graham, of Jim Brown, of Lou Groza—and, Paul Warfield says quietly, "there's my likeness." That's got to be touching, you figure. "Yes, I'm very proud of that," he says.

Yet once again, it works both ways. What Warfield draws your attention to, finally, is another figure in that mural: "The unidentified likeness of the next player in Browns history who is going to carry that new tradition forever," Warfield says. "It is still the Cleveland Browns. And that unidentified portion of the mural, in the orange helmet, represents the future star and great players who will keep this tradition going better than ever."

So you can take Paul Warfield's own line, and you can turn it right back on him. Maybe it's true about the fans, but Warf-ield shows that it's just as true about the players.

It dispelled the myth: How soon do they forget. That clearly pointed out: They don't forget. They didn't forget.

Paul Warfield didn't forget.

The Pittsburgh Game

ONE OF THE STORIES my brother and I never tire of is the Pittsburgh story, in which my father barely escapes being tossed over the second-deck railing. Like many of my father's stories, it survives in a fairly bare-bones fashion, which is the way my father tells stories. To us, it is the ultimate Cleveland–Pittsburgh story: Two blue-collar steel towns, separated by a hundred miles of turnpike; football when calling it "smash-mouth" would have been redundant. Thousands of fans from either town following their team to the rival town, so close that only a few hours' drive took you to the kickoff, so close that people living in the middle had to choose which team to root for.

The game in question took place during the late fifties, when the Pittsburgh rivalry was just taking hold. The Cleveland–Pittsburgh game was played on Saturday nights in those days, adding to the whole deal the excitement of playing under the lights.

My dad went to that game, sitting with one of his college buddies who had good seats from the company he worked for, on the 30, in the front row of the upper deck. It was a close game—rare in those days, when the Browns manhandled the Steelers most times. But still, this one was close, and the guys sitting right next to my dad and his pal wanted to see the Steelers win.

"We were in the first row watching the game, and it was an

exciting game," my dad tells me. "And the people to my left, between me and the aisle, wanted Pittsburgh. And Pittsburgh was ahead, then we went ahead, then Pittsburgh went ahead real close to the end of the game. Then we went ahead . . . and as I have been known to do I went bananas, screaming, yelling, and jumping around." It's just barely possible that my dad went a little extra bananas, knowing that Pittsburgh rooters were sitting right next to him.

This didn't go over well with the guys next to him. "They got mad at me because I was so excited," he says. "The guy sitting next to me really got pissed and grabbed me by my jacket and was ready to throw me over the edge." The guy's friend pulled him off my dad, and my dad's friend helped out too. "I switched seats with Seymour, and the guy switched seats with his friend," my dad says.

"And he got up and went after me again." The game was winding down and it was clear the Browns were going to win, so there wasn't much chance of the guy calming down. "The usher saw us," my dad says. "He suggested to us that we go up and stand in the aisle for the last couple minutes of the game." They tried that.

"Well, he got up and was still screaming and carrying on, and the usher suggested that since the Browns were obviously going to win, maybe it wasn't a bad idea for us to start walking out." They did that.

That was one of our favorite stories. Almost nothing could move our dad from his seat at a Browns game, but the Pittsburgh rivalry was so tough that even my dad left a minute or so before the end of a game to avoid being tossed on his head from the upper deck.

Cool.

And then I went to college, and in college I met a guy

named Roz who became my best friend, and he came from Pittsburgh.

And it was awful.

Our friendship wasn't awful—it was the kind of college friendship you would want for your children. We wandered the campus, we drank beer, we went on a trip and passed a long ski-lift ride singing every word of "American Pie" as a Rocky Mountain slope glided away beneath us.

But still—that Pittsburgh thing. I mean, it was something we actually discussed.

Unfortunately, the discussions usually involved me saying that I hoped he appreciated my willingness to be his friend despite his rooting interest, and his saying things like, "I wonder who the Steelers are going to play in the AFC championship game this year?" Because this was the late seventies, and things were going a little better for the Steelers than for the Browns. We were in college together for four years—for eight Cleveland–Pittsburgh games.

The Browns won once. By a point.

It was a tough time.

I remember my first Pittsburgh game in 1971. I remember noticing at home that the Sunday mood showed up around Thursday, and by Saturday the Pittsburgh game was the topic of dinner conversation and, by Sunday morning, all conversation. While she packed kaiser rolls into the grocery bag for lunch and filled the thermos, my mom would talk about the Pittsburgh game. Not because she much cared who won, but because when the Steelers were in town, that was what you talked about.

At that first Pittsburgh game, I was just starting to get it. The Browns won, and I remember Fair Hooker diving and pulling in a Bill Nelson pass that had the stadium rocking, a thing I had never before quite seen. When the game ended with the Browns in front the response was different from any other game I'd attended. There was a kind of fierce, finger-pointing celebration. Who *lost* was as important as who won. It was like the entire city of Cleveland was a big high school, and we accepted the need to beat Pittsburgh the way high schoolers just know it's important to beat Shaw or Euclid or Rocky River, and they care.

Pittsburgh games never got less intense. After the 1972 game in which Mike Phipps had his moment of glory, the Pittsburgh game was something my brother, my dad, and I would await, year after year, looking forward to it from the moment the schedule came out. My dad would tell us his up-per-deck story every year, and that became part of the ritual. In 1973 the Browns won 21–16, and that's the year Mike Phipps had his Great Escape. My dad was at that game; my brother was at the one not long after in which one play ended with Joe Greene standing above Bob McKay, kicking him in the midsection. Greene was tossed out of the game but not off the field, and he led the cheers for the Steelers the rest of the way, almost getting into a couple of other mixups before the game ended.

I was at the 18–16 victory in 1976 during which Joe "Tur-key" Jones threw Terry Bradshaw on his head and invented the "in-the-grasp" rule. That was also the first game at which I noticed the edge of violence in the stands. There weren't a lot of fights—in fact, I saw more fighting at other games—but the fans exuded a hair-trigger fierceness. Steelers fans who filled the cheap seats in the closed end of the stadium, where our season tickets were, may have grown used to their team's dominance—they had won the previous two championships and did not expect to lose. It may simply have galled them to see the Browns (coming off 3–11 and 4–10 seasons) beating them. That vicious play by Jones didn't help. Or maybe, at 16, I was finally old enough to pick up vibrations in the crowd I had never picked up before.

But I think the fact was that a Steelers game was just different. From our seats halfway up the slope of the upper deck in that closed end, we were commonly surrounded by out-of-towners—Cincinnatians, Detroiters, any number of opposing fans or groups. The second escalator ride up, to the second deck, often changed drastically in color from the brown-and-orange-clad safety of the lower deck. Still, on those escalator rides, the conversation usually continued, and you could expect to share a gentle joke with someone wearing Buffalo blue, or even a hat that said "Cincinnati" on it.

Not during the Pittsburgh game. On the way to our seats for the Pittsburgh game the majority in brown and the minority in yellow and black kept their heads down or lifted their eyes in insolent stares. We shared no jokes, enjoyed no hope-we-beat-you-guys camaraderie. During most games in those close quarters we heard plenty of inflammatory chants, and we responded with many of our own. Still, after those games, chances are the out-of-towners smiled or even shook a hand or clapped a back on their way out.

But during that 18–16 win, the chants became vicious. Beer, peanuts, cups rained down on us from the cheap seats behind. And on the way out afterwards the people who launched those missiles offered no shy, get-you-guys-next-time glances. This was the Pittsburgh game.

And then college and a best friend from Pittsburgh. To make matters worse, the Browns, of course, could not win in Pittsburgh in those years—the Three Rivers jinx lasted from 1970 to 1986, and these years were the core. Too, Roz's blithe support of the Steelers admitted of such other interests as homework, whereas my support of the Browns required that I spend every Sunday afternoon in front of the television, nervously watching for score updates. To increase the frustration, I had to watch television at Roz's house, because he had a television and I did not. This meant that I often answered the telephone and provided updates to Roz or his roommates, who often foolishly squandered their Sunday afternoons at the library, certain that they could rely on me for information.

Several ugly trends came together in 1980, during the Kardiac Kids season. Late in the season the Browns, a promising but far-from-secure 7–3, traveled to Pittsburgh to play the Steelers, a vulnerable but still threatening 6–4. The Browns had still never won at Three Rivers Stadium, and Roz and I made plans to watch the game on his TV that Sunday. When Sunday arrived, however, Roz inexplicably determined that researching a paper was more important than the Cleveland–Pittsburgh game and, making me comfortable with a bag of chips and some beer, headed to the library.

He called for updates occasionally. The game stayed close, with the Browns building and barely maintaining a 13–9 lead going into the final minutes. Naturally, with a minute or so left, the Steelers got the ball. Naturally, Roz called for an update at just about that time, which forced me to describe the last few minutes of the game to him, over the telephone.

"What's the score?" he asked.

"Thirteen to nine," I said, "with less than a minute left."

"Oh," he said, with an infuriating lack of concern. "Who has the ball?"

"You know who has the ball," I told him. "And they're driving." I watched the players line up on screen. "They're deep in Browns territory, and . . . Bradshaw has it . . . and he's scrambling . . . and . . . Roz you are my great and good friend but just now I cannot continue speaking with you," and

I slammed down the phone. This last may not be an entirely accurate transcription.

The phone rang again a moment later.

"What happened?" Roz asked. "Did they win?"

When you look at it in the right way, that telephone conversation is why Roz and I are still friends 20 years later and I'm not writing this from prison. Washington University's Olin Library can thus claim to have saved at least one life, possibly two.

But that's Cleveland–Pittsburgh. The Browns didn't win in Three Rivers stadium until 1986, when Bernie Kosar guided them to the win that ended almost two decades of failure there, and for a few months it looked like the monkey was off the Browns' backs. Later that year, of course, a brand new monkey climbed on, in a blue uniform with a "D" on the helmet, but that's another issue.

By the way, if you're looking for a lesson from that guy trying to throw my dad off the second deck, look somewhere else. I asked my dad if it affected his behavior at Browns games. "Never!" he told me. "I mean, you know in an exciting game like that, especially against Pittsburgh, I'm going to cheer." So he didn't think twice before getting season tickets to the new Browns stadium.

In the lower deck.

"For those four hours, I hated my friends"

A Moment with Greg Pruitt

 GREG PRUITT joined the Browns a year after the 1972 playoff appearance rang down the curtain on the Browns' three decades of NFL dominance. He stuck with the team through Red Right 88, which began a new generation—the heartbreak generation— of Browns fandom. This makes him perhaps the ultimate tweener—a standout performer on mostly forgettable teams, a guy who electrified the stadium in years when he pretty much had to do it all on his own.

Playing for losing teams isn't easy, but it was made easier by the dedication of Browns fans.

"They criticized us but they supported us," he says. "They had a right to. They wanted us to win, but when we didn't they were still there. People were so into football. Not from the perspective of just, 'When you gonna win a game?' but really a lot of the fans knew what they were talking about. And I had never seen so many women know about football. Not just a bunch of guys out there on Sunday not understanding what they were seeing."

That dedication evidenced itself when the Browns left Cleveland in 1995, too, Pruitt says. "It wasn't the first time a team had left a city and moved somewhere else. But it was an opportunity in tragedy to prove they loved and supported the team enough to salvage it.

"I played with Cleveland, I played with the Oakland Raiders who moved to L.A., and now I'm in Houston, where the Oilers moved to Tennessee. So I've had the experience in three different cities, or say four, including L.A. and Oakland, of watching people react to their team leaving their city. No question, the people in Cleveland showed something special, a tremendous amount of support. They got the Browns back."

And it wasn't just the fans who decried the move. Pruitt feared he had become a player without a team. Despite his years with the Raiders he'll always consider himself a Brown, and "as a player you hate to see a team leave because of the history and tradition, so many years down the drain. I have met guys from the Baltimore Colts who shared that emptiness, that feeling of helplessness, of betrayal. You know, 'My era in football is gone. The Baltimore Colts don't exist anymore.' I was very disappointed that I had fallen in with that group of guys."

Now that the Browns are back, Pruitt is free to enjoy his associations with the team again, and nothing, he says—nothing—was like one particular part of being a Brown.

"People ask me to compare playing in college and pro," he says. College students have so much energy and school spirit, Pruitt says, that "I don't think there's a comparison between the enthusiasm of college and pro."

Well, *almost* no comparison.

"The exception to me was when Cleveland played Pittsburgh. The enthusiasm was unbelievable." He remembers his first Monday-night game in Cleveland against the Dolphins—the same one Paul Warfield remembered—and the feeling of support he got from the fans. "You got the feeling that if you could give them your uniform, they would play." He thought that was as powerful as professional fan support could get.

And then came Pittsburgh.

"Well, the mood in our practices changed," he recalls. "I noticed—coaches were like we can't do this, we can't do that. Their whole demeanor changed."

And then came the game. "Leroy Kelly was there, it was 1973, and I got a chance to play right at the end. We were ahead, we were behind, and I went in for the winning touchdown."

The fans stormed the field after the game, he says. "Then it hit me—man, this must be an important game, because they didn't do this last Sunday." As the crowd increased, he got lost in his thoughts for a moment: "It hit me, 'I just figured out I'm going to be on TV. I ran the winning touchdown,' I'm a rookie, I'm going over in my head what I'm going to say. . . ."

And then he looked up and he was surrounded. "People came on the field, they were trying to pat me on the head, which is fine . . . but when you've got ten thousand people trying to pat you on the head you start to get worried." As the crowd crushed in, in fact, he got worried enough that he started hustling pretty hard to find that welcoming door to the dugout tunnel. "Finally I saw it, and I started to trot to it. Once I got beyond the guards, I could slow down."

He started collecting his thoughts again as he slowly made his way through the tunnel towards the locker room, rehearsing his comments for the TV cameras. "All the time, I'm walking up this ramp. And then I get to the top and open the door.

"And I walk into the Pittsburgh locker room."

In the chaos, Pruitt had ducked into the wrong dugout. And

there he stood, in the doorway of a room full of extremely annoyed men in black and gold. "I walk in and Noll was there and he was screaming and hollering at these guys, and I was like, 'Oops, sorry . . .'" So he backed out.

"And the fans were at one end and Pittsburgh was at the other. There was nowhere to go."

So Greg Pruitt hung around the tunnel for fifteen minutes or so until the crowd thinned out and he could safely make it across the field to his own tunnel and his own locker room, which he did—too late to be on TV, too late to take his first bow as a Browns star.

"But that's my fondest memory," he says—a memory of fans so supportive, so demonstrative, that they were as fearsome as the 1973 Pittsburgh Steelers.

The Pittsburgh game never got less intense in his eight years with the Browns. Every year the practices changed, every year everything somehow got turned up a click.

"Usually you leave the rivalry and the bragging and the threats and whatever between the fans," Pruitt says. "It was a business with us. We played our hardest, but usually we were friends before the game, after the game, and usually during the game. I had a lot of friends that played on the Pittsburgh team.

"But for some reason, the Pittsburgh–Cleveland games . . ." he hesitates. "Man, we hated Pittsburgh. For those four hours, I hated my friends."

Red Right 88

I came home from college for the 1980 winter break to find the city in madness. "That record of the 'Twelve Days of a Browns Christmas?'" my mom said. "I wanted to get you that but you can't get it, as fast as they put them on the shelves that's how fast they sell."

Just as well. In the first place, I didn't really want a record—what I wanted was a ticket to a playoff game. In the second place, there was the small matter of the last regular-season game against Cincinnati that had to be won before talk of the playoffs at the stadium became reasonable.

But truly, the city was mad for the Browns, mad in a way I had never seen it. I had grown up during the "We want Phipps" years and the bottoming out shortly thereafter, and I had been away at college for the falls during which Brian Sipe had begun weaving his magic spell—which had never, so far, been quite magical enough. I remembered watching him lead the Browns to a 26–7 defeat of the Cowboys on a Monday night the year before, after which the Browns were 4–0 and talking big. By the time I was settled abroad, where I spent the rest of that year, I received a letter from my dad telling me the Browns had stumbled to 4–3; they finished out of the money. So as far as I was concerned, nothing was certain yet.

But when we gathered in my aunt's den to watch that Cincinnati game, something was different. We all took our regular roles—my stepfather's Eeyore doom and gloom, my uncle's perverse swings from wild optimism to insane pessimism, my brother's wild overreactions to questionable playcalling or seeming malfeasance by officials, my own fearful, nervous hopefulness, followed by a hesitant ebullience even after a score, when before shouting in glee I would make sure that enough time had passed so that a flag just could not fall to ruin everything. Best was my cousin Scott's campy Jewish grand-mother–style nonstop chatter, referring to team members as though they were his children, giving them nicknames. His fa-vorite that year was Lyle Alzado, whose name he pronounced as though the man were named Zeta—Al Zeta. "Al Zeta!" he'd shout when Alzado made a tackle or stuffed a run. "Al Zeta, my Zeta!" He brought a friend along to increase the noise. My dad watched at his own house, and we chatted by phone during halftime.

The game swung back and forth, never looking safe for the Browns, and for many anxious moments looking like a sure last-second loss. But these were the Kardiac Kids, after all; they had been winning games in the last seconds for two years, and it appeared the gods had them lined up for this year's play-offs. Finally, excruciatingly, the Bengals went down, fighting to the end, and the gun sounded and the Browns were Cen-tral Division champs for the first time since I had seen them clinch the division against these same Bengals in 1971, when I had worried that my uncle Sam might leap so crazily that he would tumble down the sloping stadium seats. This time Sam was jumping around just as much—so were we all—but I didn't worry about him hurting himself on a La-Z-Boy or a sofa, so I just enjoyed the moment.

"Okay!" my cousin's friend shouted. "Let's go scream in the streets!"

And for the only time in my life, we did. We ran out, sock-footed, into the snow, jumping around for just a moment or two. A couple other doors on my aunt's suburban street opened up, smiling people stepping out to offer a tentative holler. But the moment lasted only briefly. For one thing, we had to rush inside to watch the postgame show. For another, this was only prelude. The playoffs awaited.

No Browns fan—no Clevelander—needs to be reminded of the delirium surrounding that playoff game. I dragged a hungover friend to the May Company to await the opening of their Ticketron machine the day tickets went on sale, waited for several hours sweating in a winter coat, and went home empty handed. But I was in college then, and I didn't believe that tickets I truly wanted could evade my grasp, and I made calls—I looked at ads, I called ticket agencies, I called friends, I networked.

No dice. And it looked, unimaginably, like I would be watching the Browns play the Raiders on television.

And then, marvelously, the cold.

And what cold. Cold from Canada, cold over the lake, cold like even Cleveland did not get often. Cold with wind that drove the chill factor down into the negative thirties. Cold that could be expected to freeze the Raiders, used to balmy California.

Best of all, cold that would keep at least a few less-dedicated fans at home. Which was why a man connected to my mother's place of work called her the day before the game and asked if I was still looking for tickets, and why I ended up on the Shaker Rapid the morning of the game with my stepfather, my best friend, his father, and a big thermos of hot cocoa that my mother's friend had forced on us when we picked up the tickets that morning. It turned out that thermos leaked all over us the entire game.

Oh, but that Rapid Transit ride. Packed together in our brown and orange ski caps and our mittens we still froze on the barely heated train cars, and we screamed for the Browns: "Who's gonna win?" we asked, and we answered ourselves. We poured from the Terminal Tower, we streamed over the West Third Street Bridge, we found our unfamiliar seats in the lower deck, around the 30 on the closed end of the field. We discovered that we were covered with cocoa. We discovered that long before kickoff we were very cold indeed.

And then we watched the game.

Frozen to the bone, hands dropped passes; cleats failed to find purchase on the icy field. An interception return for a touchdown put the Browns up 6–0, but in the windswept open end of the stadium the extra point off the toe of Don Cockroft, the last of the great straight-on kickers, fluttered wide, ominously.

Halftime came and we froze. We tried to drink liquor, but we still froze. The cocoa dripped on our pants legs and froze. Still, it was like heaven, and I drank in the feeling like ambrosia. In the brittle air the stadium didn't boom and rumble the way it usually did—rather it crackled, hissed, buzzed.

The game went on. The Raiders scored twice, and the Browns put two field goals through in the closed end of the stadium, finding themselves down 14–12 with a minute or so to go. They got the ball.

And then here came the Kardiac Kids. Suddenly everything was different—passes found soft hands, running backs found holes. And 77,000 people seemed to awaken as one: A storybook season, it appeared, would have a storybook ending. The fans believed. The broadcasters believed. The players believed. The stadium vibrated as though it would rattle itself into the lake.

And for once in my life I missed it completely.

I didn't believe. Part of it was a big, ugly reality check. Yeah, you came back on the Green Bay Packers, on the Baltimore

Colts, on the Houston Oilers. But those guys across the line today? Those were the Oakland Raiders over there, and they weren't a bunch you did a lot of sneaky things to in those days.

Plus, it was freezing and nasty and everything was wrong with the weather, and the Browns had played like hell all day and maybe I had a million other reasons but the fact is, when I saw that team making its way down the field, I just thought to myself, "Nope. Not our guys; nuh-unh. This doesn't come to us."

Maybe it was the wind, or two missed field goals and a missed extra point, or six fumbles or two other interceptions. It could have been my negative vibes.

But I prefer to think it was karma, and that one minute ahead of everybody else I recognized it: the Browns my dad had rooted for were forever in the past, and me and these Browns, well, we hadn't yet paid our dues, not by a long shot.

If you think about it, this was about the first time in their history—more than 30 years at that point—that a good Browns team could have been considered a surprise. The 1970s had been the first decade in which the Browns had not won at least one championship—and the first decade in which they had not played for at least *four*. The seventies, no picnic anywhere, were the first rotten decade for the Cleveland Browns. And suddenly, in 1980, there Browns fans were again, only 16 years since our last championship, acting as though it had been 50 years, as though we had been suffering for decades.

I think that's bad karma. Browns fans had had a ride like no other, had enjoyed success that no football team had ever before enjoyed. Even that great Packers team was only a dynasty for eight years—but the Browns had gone on for three decades, and after our first brief drought we thought we were dying of thirst. I think Browns fans were arrogant.

And I think the gods hate that—and I think they punished

us. I think that if we were going to act like we had suffered they were going to show us some suffering. For years, rooting for the Browns had been what Paul Brown had wanted it to be— like rooting for the New York Yankees. I believe the gods at that moment, angered by the fans' arrogance, turned on a dime and said, "No more!" From that moment on the Browns would never again be football's equivalent of the Yankees. From then on they would be the Yankees' polar opposite: From that last, frozen drive in January 1981, the Browns would be football's answer to the Boston Red Sox.

The gods were going to make us suffer like Red Sox fans. The Red Sox lose close, lose heartbreakers. Red Right 88? That was a Red Sox loss. It's coming so close that hurts, and that 1981 game was as close as a game can be, and the loss hurt as much as a loss can hurt. I think that 1981 game started a new era for Browns rooters—an era of excruciating losses. Red Right 88 opened the door for the Drive, the Fumble. Think of how many seasons of NFL teams are defined by a single word, or two: the Immaculate Reception of the Steelers and Raiders in 1972; the Catch of the 49ers and Cowboys in 1981. The only others are the Browns: Red Right 88, the Drive, the Fumble. There are few times when a single play or series defines an entire game, an entire season for a team or two. And for the Browns, since 1980, that's happened three times, and all for the worst. Nobody else in the league comes close to that.

I think we need to face it: As fans, it was our turn. We needed those painful losses.

And how painful was Red Right 88? As usual, fans forget some of the harsher realities of that moment, much the way some people prefer to remember that had Bill Buckner fielded that ground ball the Red Sox would have won the 1986 World Series. Well, they wouldn't. Had Buckner fielded that ball, the Red Sox would have escaped into extra innings, on the road, against a Mets team that had come back from two runs down with two outs in the ninth—against a team that believed. The Red Sox certainly would have lost. The loss was coming—Buckner just had the shoulders broad enough to carry the load.

Same in the arctic, windswept open end of Cleveland Municipal Stadium on January 4, 1981. "He didn't need to throw that pass," people say of Sipe's errant toss into the end zone—either forgetting or plain ignoring that Don Cockroft had missed two short field goals and an extra point in that open end of the stadium and the Browns needed a touchdown. Maybe Cockroft was going to suddenly find his leg at the end of this worst of all days for straight-on kickers, but my money—all of our money—was on Brian Sipe, the miracle worker who had brought us here. The ground was uncertain—Mike Pruitt, Greg Pruitt, and Calvin Hill had combined for 82 yards all game—and that left only one option. Brian Sipe was going to have to find one more magic spell in that shoulder of his.

Did the Raiders know that, and look for the pass? Or was the loss just was coming anyway, and the gods just found the shoulders broad enough to bear it?

Anyhow, Sipe threw the pass, Mike Davis of the Raiders got to it before Ozzie Newsome did, and the game was over. We all remember the moment. Greg Pruitt, on the sidelines for that play, says he was standing with his toes under a heater, facing away from the field, wondering what the parties were going to be like that night, when he saw the eyes of the players he was facing widen. "Did you ever see *The Longest Yard?*" he asks. That play seemed to take as long as the last play in the movie. "From that moment everything went in slow motion," he says. He spun, saw Sipe drop back; saw the pass; saw Davis muscle in for it. "There was a lot of cheering," Pruitt says. "And all of a sudden you could hear a dime drop."

All of a sudden it was over.

And all of a sudden it meant something different to be a fan of the Cleveland Browns. For years it was easy—Browns fans could have been called front-runners. How hard was it to root for a team that played for the championship every other year, and won plenty of those games? How hard was it to root for a team that had virtually invented the modern game of football? Rooting for the Browns until the sixties was exactly what Paul Brown had wanted it to be like: it was like rooting for the New York Yankees. Red Right 88 showed that it was never going to be like that again.

During the seventies Browns fans learned disappointment, but that's easy too—you've got to expect some downtime after 30 years of success. So when the teams were terrible in the mid-seventies, Browns fans could simply look forward to the next dynasty, and when the late-seventies teams started winning, it all seemed to be coming back.

Then this—and maybe it wasn't going to be so easy after all. No, suddenly Browns fans knew not merely disappointment—suddenly Browns fans knew heartbreak.

I maintain that we needed that heartbreak—that heartbreak tempers fandom. During the seventies, the front-runners, if there were any, dropped off. From Red Right 88 on, those of us who came up after the championships forged our support and made it stronger, and our love of the Browns became deeper and more maniacal for those disappointments. When the next championship comes, we'll enjoy it all the more for Red Right 88 and after, for all the close calls—the heartbreaking closeness of Red Right 88 makes us stronger.

Pruitt has another story about Red Right 88. A year later he found himself playing for the Raiders. "The guy that intercepted that ball was Mike Davis," Pruitt says. "The very next year I'm in the Raiders' camp. We're in 8-on-8 drills—no line, just receivers and defensive backs." In this low-key drill passes were tossed short, long, and everywhere else. Defensive backs caught them as often as receivers. Well, all the defensive backs except one: "In 80 degrees, perfect weather, this guy couldn't catch the ball," Pruitt says of Davis. Balls dropped off his shoulders, off his jersey, off his hands. "He couldn't catch a cold!"

Pruitt finally held up his hands and stopped practice. In that famous game, under those terrible conditions, an interception beat the Browns. "This is the guy who made that play?" Pruitt asked his new teammates of the guy who couldn't catch the ball. "This guy caught that ball in extreme conditions and he can't catch the ball now?" The players laughed. "So I said, well it just wasn't meant to be then." And they got on with practice.

It just wasn't meant to be.

That's a lot of talk, and I can't claim we all knew what was happening in that icy stadium on January 4, 1981. But the fans walked out silently into the snow, wheezing and blowing as we shuffled back to our cars and the Rapid, and we knew we had seen something. Few fans, drunk or angry, bellowed or cursed. It was a moment of introspection. Something had happened, and we had been there. As we headed through the frozen city to our homes, we could only wait to see what would come next.

Almostness

A Moment with Brian Sipe

SO YOU'RE TALKING with Brian Sipe, because you're working on a project for which he's been mentioned. It has nothing to do with football. You have your conversation, you finish your discussion. Sipe has been nice, articulate in that way that people who don't consider themselves articulate can be. You're chatting about this and that, and it's coming to time to hang up. You hesitate.

Then, suddenly, out with it. You've interviewed plenty of people before—athletes, celebrities, elected officials, Nobel Prize winners, but . . . but this is Brian Sipe. "I never do this," you tell him. "But I have to. I hate to bother you with this, but I grew up in Cleveland, and I'm a big Browns fan. And I just wanted to say: You know, 1980?" Silence, but you forge ahead. "Thanks for that," you say. "Just . . . thanks."

A moment passes, and you cringe. "Oh, jeez," you figure. "He gets this all the time, people stumbling all over themselves, he must be sick of it, oh you big dummy, why couldn't you just leave the guy in peace?"

And then he answers, his voice warm. "Yeah," he says. "We had fun, didn't we?"

That inclusive "we" shows to what depth Brian Sipe is Brown. He doesn't talk about the team, he doesn't talk about

73

himself, he doesn't talk about how great he was—don't forget, he was the MVP that year—or how disappointed he was when that pass was intercepted and when, after that miraculous year, the magic just never returned. No, what he remembers is fun, and fun that he shared with his teammates and with the entire city of Cleveland.

"That was a special time," he says. And not a time he expected. Growing up in Southern California, where the L.A. Dodgers fans who leave in the seventh inning are considered the loyal ones, he says, "I was completely unprepared for not only the attention but the genuine caring, the sort of identification they had with the team as being part of their family. In San Diego, the fan support was based primarily on what your win-loss record was. If you win, people come out and see you and if you don't there are other things for them to do."

And then Sipe started playing for a team that was 3–11 and played in front of 70,000 people.

He loved that support—though Sipe also would have liked to be able to eat a meal without being asked for autographs or badgered for comment. "But at the same time that I wanted to protect my privacy," he says, "the people who weren't honoring it were so genuine and so darn nice that I really couldn't feel any anger." As his career went on, he compared his experience with those of players elsewhere—Jim McMahon in Chicago, for example.

"On the one hand I kind of respected the fact that he was his own person," Sipe says. "On the other, it was obvious to me that he didn't have the same regard for the people of Chicago, and they for him, that us Browns players had for our fans, and they for us."

And so as much as the city of Cleveland roots for the Browns, Sipe now returns the favor. "I'm always very proud to be part of it," he says. "I'm a fan of the city of Cleveland. I find myself rooting for that town in a way that I didn't think was possible."

No, growing up in San Diego you wouldn't think that was possible. It's just different in Cleveland, and it always was, and never more so than the day after that devastating loss to the Raiders in 1981. Sipe was named Most Valuable Player of the NFL that day, though it didn't mean much to him at the time. "I could think of no higher public honor, and yet I was more in the mood to sort of fall on my sword after what had happened out at the stadium."

Still, persuaded by his wife to join some friends for a dinner commitment of long standing, he went out to dinner. "I didn't want to be out and about and have to talk to Browns fans," he recalls. "I remember walking into the restaurant, and hoping it was dark, wondering if it was possible to sneak into the corner where I hoped our table was."

Yeah, right. The door opened, and every eye in the restaurant snapped to Brian Sipe. "I was at a loss," Sipe recalls.

First, a moment of stunned silence.

"And then the room spontaneously broke into applause. It absolutely floored me. To me . . . nothing about my growing up in San Diego prepared me for that."

With their applause, with their support, with their plain affection, Browns fans had started Sipe on the road to a realization that still stuns him to this day: that Red Right 88, with its heartbreak and loss and disappointment, has enriched him—has enriched us all—maybe even more than a win in that game would have.

At the banquet at which he received his MVP award, a writer told Sipe that it might be hard to believe, but the wrenching loss might turn out to be more memorable, in his own life and in the lives of his teammates and fans, than a win would have been. "In time, it would become a sweeter moment, is the gist of what he told me.

"Well, it has. I think as I look back on that season that there's only really two ways that season could have ended and left us all feeling as close as we did—and that was to have made it to the Super Bowl and won in Kardiac fashion, or to have what happened."

That is, to come to your unforgettable denouement in front of 77,000 of your closest friends. To be with people who think you're family. To face your moment of passion and glory and madness in the frenzy of that gray, embracing stadium.

And then—if it wasn't going to work, at least to have that one last drive, that one final moment. "It's not like we were knocking on the door all day long, or it was a high-scoring game," Sipe says. "I mean, I was calling plays based on what the ground was like underneath the huddle because that's where I'd be setting up. I knew I couldn't run a sweep, because Greg Pruitt wouldn't be able to cut upfield.

"It was most unlikely that having everything gone wrong all day long that we had suddenly mustered all the intangibles that had earmarked the season and found ourselves poised for a miracle."

But they did. And if the miracle just didn't quite come off, maybe it was the *almostness* of the moment that made it so sweet.

"The worst thing that could have happened would have been to have it go down in a whimper," he says. "As I look back on it, it was a little bit like a Shakespeare play—it really ended in the most exciting way. Suddenly, when it mattered, everything came together.

"And you know what? There was an expectation among all of us that it was going to. It was pretty remarkable." For one unforgettable minute, it was all going to happen, and we were all there. We were all going to be part of it. And yes, it was bitter that it didn't, but yes, certainly, it's sweet that it almost did. "There was a hopefulness about it," Sipe recalls. "I think even in the kind of pain of the 1980 ending, there was a hopefulness about what was going to happen in the future. Because we had been so close. It appeared as if it was in our grasp." And if that turned out not to be the case, how much sweeter was the moment for that belief?

And so Brian Sipe doubles back and once again asks that wonderful, inclusive question: "We had fun, didn't we?"

You damn betcha.

Diaspora

AT ABOUT THIS TIME—the beginning of the 1980s—two contrasting trends were redefining the city of Cleveland. One was the continued exodus of people, industries, and jobs that had been bleeding the city for two decades.

The other was the good-natured, Midwestern courage demonstrated by those left behind. They started nursing that beat-up little town back to health, and damned if it didn't start to work. The river got cleaner; so did the lake. Not a fire on either in more than a decade, and George Voinovich just wasn't the type to set his hair on fire. Once the smoke cleared, people seemed to see better. In cleaning up the financial mess left behind by Dennis Kucinich, Mayor Voinovich started a tradition of the mayor working along with the city council, something unheard of in Cleveland for decades. Business leaders rolled up their sleeves. Deals were done. Everywhere new growth began in the city.

And suddenly, the good Clevelanders who had sadly moved on to seek their fortunes elsewhere, barely glancing back in their rearview mirrors at a city broke, filthy, and hopeless, began to look backward with a little more longing. First, of course, they looked Clevelandward with little more than the glow of nostalgia. But then, bit by bit, they began to hold Cleveland up for admiration with genuine pride.

I say "they," of course, but I mean "we."

I had left Cleveland in 1977 to go off to college, but after college there was plainly no reason to return. I wandered here and there, but as I did I learned that wherever I lived I carried a specific identity: I was the guy from Cleveland.

At first that meant self-deprecating jokes. "Cleveland is a great place to be from," I would say, emphasizing the act of abandoning our downtrodden town. But I never lost that feeling of Cleveland in my bones. "Cleveland: You've got to be tough," a T-shirt around in the seventies used to say, and I always felt a little of that native toughness resided even in me, a suburban boy whose entire downtown experience took place between the stadium and the Arcade. I moved around, living in towns where two inches of forecast snow had people scrambling to the supermarket to stock up on canned goods, and I started to take a little pride in being from a place where if it snowed a foot, people recognized that stuff just happened sometimes—a lot of snow, an abandoned factory, a burning river, or even a trashed neighborhood—and you just had to do something about it and carry on.

So when I started to see Cleveland hustling around cleaning up its act, I started to bristle a little at all those Cleveland jokes, and I stopped making them myself. Every time I came back to town—often to see the Browns—it became clearer how much I had left behind.

And then, as years went by, something else became clear: I hadn't left it behind.

Everywhere ex-Clevelanders get together you hear it—that nostalgic, proud sense of connection. We still say Cleveland's a good place to be from, but now we emphasize the town, not the distance. Maybe it was just one burning river joke too many. It's like having a drunken family member or an irritating friend: You can make all the jokes you want to, but let someone else try it and just see how things go.

Whatever the reason, somehow, all the Cleveland alumni

felt a bond, and at meetings or when traveling I always found myself having loving conversations about Corky & Lenny's or Edgewater Park with somebody I'd never seen before. We'd immediately ask one another the obvious question—"Oh, yeah? East Side or West Side?"—and then try to ignore the answer if it was wrong. Like all expatriates, we couldn't fail to bring with us part of what we thought we were escaping.

And the Browns somehow ran right through the middle of it. We never talked about the Indians, we never talked about the Cavaliers—but we always talked about the Browns.

Still, for years I didn't think much about the Browns as part of that Cleveland identity. Because though my Cleveland identity was rather lost and found, my identity with the Browns had never wavered. I stood up for them in college, I rooted for them from Europe, I wanly cheered them from San Diego and Philadelphia, though I always did so alone or with a few understanding but puzzled local friends.

And, really, I thought that despite our shared Cleveland heritage, this business with the Browns was just me, or maybe just me and my brother.

But that was before I met Harold Manson.

Out of Town Brown

A Moment with Harold Manson

I FIRST LAID EYES on Harold Manson in a New York bar in the 1980s. I was visiting my sister, and the Browns were playing an exhibition game, and my sister said that our cousin Amy was organizing some sort of Browns club that was meeting at some bar somewhere. So we went and there was Harold Manson.

Harold Manson, visiting New York from San Jose, California, had made it a point to find the bar showing the Browns game so he didn't miss this game. An exhibition game.

Now this was a whole new order of things, as far as I was concerned.

Harold wore a T-shirt with the Browns' schedule on it, and at the end of the season it showed the Browns with an appointment for the Super Bowl. Of course we all know they didn't make it, but that's not the point. The point was that Harold Manson felt about the Browns the way I did, and he was doing something about it. And so was my cousin Amy.

This was, it turned out, my introduction to the Browns Backers.

I felt like I had found my tribe. I wasn't psychotic, as my friends and spouse thought. Or at least—it wasn't just me. I took Harold's name and address, and I vowed to call him.

Harold Manson turned out to be the president of the Bay Area Browns Backers. He had grown up in Houston, in the 1930s and 1940s. He had traveled the world in the military.

And he had never seen a single game in Cleveland Stadium. Yet cut Harold Manson and he bleeds Cleveland Brown.

"Let me tell you how mine starts," Harold says of his story as a Browns fan. "Mine starts with me in Catholic school in a Christmas play, dressed up as an elf. I'm the original elf!" That was in the 1930s, and the Browns didn't exist. But Harold Manson looks back and sees the connection—and the newsletter that BABB sends out even now uses that famous Browns brownie in its logo.

Of course, Manson waited until the Browns actually existed before becoming a big fan, but he got started in their first year. "In 1946 I was in eighth grade, and by that time we had started reading the newspaper. There was no NFL or AAFC in Houston, but we found that the team in the AAFC that was beating up on everybody was the Browns. And they had this fullback, Motley, and whoa! That was it. He was running back supreme."

So in after-school football games, everybody running the ball was Marion Motley, everyone throwing the ball was Otto Graham. "We had as a football a tin can wrapped in a paper bag," he says. "It wasn't because of poverty. I think it was because it was so light you could grab it in one hand and fly away with it—it was easy to handle." The easier, of course, to be Dante "Gluefingers" Lavelli.

This was in Texas, where football had meant high-school ball—"It wasn't until I was in college that I found out about the Detroit Thanksgiving game," he says. "That didn't mean anything. That was pro—that was minor-league stuff to us." But somehow the Browns broke through.

One reason was the Browns Radio Network, on which he and his friends could hear Browns games. But mostly, he says, the Browns were just the class of the league, the class of pro football, and somehow the connection was made. "They were winners," he says.

In 1951 Manson went to college, in Missouri, to study journalism. He headed straight for the journalism library and found that the school received all the major papers in the nation—"And lo and behold I found the *Plain Dealer*. I said, 'I've died and gone to heaven!'" The papers from his hometown of Houston didn't make it to the library, but Manson didn't worry. "Why would I want to read about something at home when I had the *Plain Dealer* to read?"

He laughs. "That's when I really realized what a fanatic I was."

When he graduated college he went into the army, "and it seems like everyplace I went in the army, the Special Services library always had the *PD*. I went to Germany, and there was the *Plain Dealer*. So I continued my ritual—every third or fourth day, reading the *PD*. Then finally they sent me to Korea, and I figured, that's it. And I went to the library—and there was the *PD*! I said, 'Somebody up there is taking care of me.'"

In 1960 a new team, the Oilers, had come to Houston, but that didn't make much of an impression on Harold Manson. "I was in Germany reading the *Plain Dealer*, so what did I care about the Houston Oilers?"

Manson ended his career in the service and moved to San Jose in 1975, where he's been ever since. But one day in 1985, at his administrative job at San Jose State, he overheard a clerk mention a sports bar, where they played all kinds of football games on TV every week. He had never heard of the concept, but he went to check it out.

"I said, well, this could be something big! And at the same time I heard about the Southern California Browns Backers—

Browns News Illustrated said they were watching the Browns games down there. So I put the two together."

And Harold Manson flew down to Los Angeles to watch a Browns game. "There was some excuse, I had to go down there," he laughs, but he went down and he watched the Browns play Buffalo. "Then two weeks later I found another excuse to go." And while he was down there he learned of a trip the club was planning to make to Seattle to see the Browns play in person.

He went. "It was the first time in my whole life! And it was awesome." He remembers best being there on Saturday before the game and seeing some of the players in their hotel. "I was stunned," he says. "This is real. They are real people, without the football togs on. I had never thought of them that way."

Before long, of course, Manson organized his own Browns Backers club, putting notices in the newspaper. For the first planned game, "one guy showed up with his son, and the bar couldn't get the game." Undaunted, Manson kept it up, eventually getting the *Browns News Illustrated* mailing list. "When we finished in 1995 we had 500 members," he says—200 are still active members of a club that hasn't had a team to root for in three years. They took over 11 Bay Area bars. Manson and others have gone to see games in San Francisco, San Diego, Phoenix, Houston, and Kansas City.

But never yet in Cleveland. "I'm saving that for something," he smiles. "I don't know what." His Browns Backers members kept threatening to send Manson to Cleveland. "But after I got the club organized, it was more interesting to me to be here."

Members of the Browns have come to talk to his group— Clay Matthews, Brian Sipe, Jerry Sherk. He's suffered through Red Right 88—"That one really hurt bad because he didn't have to do it"—and the Drive. "That was bad—you know why? Because we were in our place—that same place I invited people to and nobody showed up. The local ABC affiliate came up to me and said 'How do you feel about winning this game?' and I said, 'We're finally going to the Super Bowl!' That really hurt."

But what Harold Manson says will always define that special Browns feeling for him is a meeting he had with a priest who used to live in Sandusky. When he lived in the Cleveland area, he told Manson, "he was able to get Browns tickets for all the kids he could drive up there, even when the game was sold out. I think that kind of caring for people just goes down through the years, the Browns loving them, them loving the Browns."

Manson likens his feelings about the Browns to feelings for a woman: "It's the kind of affair you just can't quit," he says.

It was a long three years without her. Harold Manson is glad she's back.

He Chose Us

 My BROTHER AND I watched the 1984 Hail Mary game between Boston College and the University of Miami on television in the family room of my mom's University Heights home while my mom slept on the couch. As amazing pass followed amazing pass we kept jumping up, shaking our arms, and hopping around the room—silently, because we didn't want to wake her: dancing on tiptoe in stocking feet, engaging in silent hand slaps, miming amazed screams. Periodically we had to run into the living room to say out loud how remarkable it was, what we were watching. Like the rest of the country we were focused on that tiny Flutie and amazed at what he was accomplishing. Yet before that final pass, when Kosar had brought his Miami team back one more time, making Flutie's efforts seem all for naught, we had to say that this Kosar looked pretty remarkable himself. Then came Flutie's last-second Hail Mary touchdown, and we hopped and jumped and boogied in the family room while my mom still slept through our idiotic football gyrations.

It was nothing she hadn't slept through before.

So when I first heard that this Kosar fellow was skating around the edges of all kinds of different rules to engineer his supplemental draft by the Cleveland Browns because he had rooted for them his whole life and wanted to play for them that badly, I was pretty pleased.

No—I was surprised. This was 1984, don't forget. In 1984, nobody was doing dances about coming to Cleveland. Only a year before, John Elway had done a dance about not wanting to go to Baltimore, and he had successfully manipulated a trade to Denver for himself. Many Clevelanders saw what Elway did and feared that it was only a matter of time before someone did the same to Cleveland, which after all was an awful lot like Baltimore—a fading, tired, Rust Belt city without much to recommend it, at least not from afar. Things were changing a little, but there wasn't anything much you could point to just yet.

No, Cleveland wasn't winning any beauty contests in 1984. The last thing Cleveland had had to cheer about, in fact, was that 1980 Browns team, which after all that bittersweet hopefulness had become the 1981 Browns (5–11), which led to the strike year, Brian Sipe's disappointing final year, and the 1984 Browns (5–11). The fans still supported the team, of course, but it looked like a long time before any player would be desperate to join the roster.

And then here came Kosar. He grew up in Boardman, Ohio, rooting for the Browns; always wanted to be a Brown; and then, given the opportunity, he chose it. He chose Cleveland.

He chose us.

It was kind of stunning. It was like being the geek in junior high school and all of a sudden the coolest person in school— the quarterback, for crying out loud—comes and sits right at your table at lunch. He talks to you. He treats you like you exist. He treats you like you count for something. He says he'd like to come over and play ball some time, if that would be okay with you. Everyone else in the world was at best ignoring Cleveland, more likely still cracking jokes that had been old for 10 years. But Bernie Kosar wanted Cleveland—and he probably would have wanted it even if it weren't changing.

And then Kosar added something else to the puzzle. A friend of mine has told me that the thing about Kosar, the thing that made him perfect for the Browns of the eighties, was that he looked so damned awkward out there. He looked like one of us. Greg Pruitt said he felt that if he gave them uniforms, the Browns fans would have played—that's how much they cared. Kosar looked like someone had. A gawky guy with a weird throwing motion who couldn't hardly run, Kosar looked exactly like some nice accounting major who had won a contest and got to pull on a uniform for a game. He looked exactly like one of us would have looked out there—a little unsteady, a little goofy, but with a heart the size of the football he held.

And then, from the start, he won. Sure, his first year—1985—the Browns stumbled into the playoffs, losing their last game and making the postseason only because nobody else in the division won as many games as they lost. No matter—the Browns were in the playoffs, where they briefly looked like they might steal a game from the Dolphins. More important, Kosar believed. You could see it from the way he stood over center. You could see it in the way he barked out plays, directed his teammates, made his awkward throws look authoritative. He clearly believed in himself.

Cleveland hadn't experienced this in a while, and it felt good. In fact, from there it radiated outward: He believe not just in himself but in his team, and, somehow, by proxy, in the city. It was kind of contagious, this belief, and it started to spread. It wasn't long before the playoff games—and even a few playoff wins, the first since, if you can believe it, 1969—started proving that Kosar knew something we didn't. He believed in us before we believed in ourselves.

But for those of us who grew up in Cleveland in the sixties and seventies—those of us who left, and those of us who remained behind—the playoff victories, the playoffs themselves, were extra. What Bernie Kosar brought to Cleveland was believing: wanting to be in Cleveland, coming to Cleveland, choosing Cleveland.

Which was a whole new chapter in being Brown.

"All I remember is being a Browns fan"

A Moment with Bernie Kosar

IF WE VIEW BERNIE KOSAR as a civic hero as much as a sports hero, it turns out we're exactly right. Yes, Bernie Kosar wanted to play for the Browns, but it was the city as much as the team that Kosar chose, the setting as much as the jewel.

"Well, you know I was obviously a huge Browns fan," Kosar says from his Miami office, "and my father used to take me to the games. I wanted the opportunity not only to go back and play for the Browns, but the bigger issue of it was wanting to live in that part of the country. To live in Cleveland. I grew up as a Youngstown guy, a Cleveland guy, and I wanted to live there. I had my family and friends there, and it made it a great situation."

And yes, this was long before the city was coming back, before people started writing about Cleveland as an example of how to fix a broken city. "Cleveland has really had an unbelievable renaissance over the last 15 years," Kosar says. "The city today is one of the most beautiful cities in the whole country. I don't think many people could have made that statement in 1984. But it wasn't about the cosmetic changes. I just like the area, the people.

"I grew up in a steelworkers' town, and I didn't have a high-maintenance lifestyle, nor did I have the expectation of making tons of money. So yeah, I could have gone to other cities or other teams or other markets and made significantly more money, but I was making more money playing pro football than I ever could have imagined, so that was enough."

That was enough—that, of course, and playing for the team that he started rooting for as kid. What game, what moment cemented him as a Browns fan?

"I don't know if anything ever really solidified it," he says. "I just have always been one. All I remember is being a Browns fan. Going to those Browns–Steelers games, Browns–Bengals games, growing up in Youngstown, being dead square between the two cities. Those memories of [how] your Monday morning feelings were directly correlated to what happened Sunday between one and four o'clock."

So what was it like, coming out of that tunnel for the first time—a lifetime of rooting for the guys coming out there, and then here he was, one of them? Did he have a moment of recognition, say to himself that he was part of something profound?

"I didn't say that when it first happened," he recalls. "I felt so much responsibility to perform and do well, I didn't have time to reflect and feel good about everything. I was so focused on what I had to do, to not let people down, not let my teammates down, not let the fans down. I had such a focus, such a concentration level, not too much got in the way of me focusing on how to win."

Still, that moment coming out of the tunnel is something he'll never forget. "I have a picture hanging in my house of me and Ozzie coming out of the tunnel before the Jets double-overtime game. I'm not going to do a good job of articulating the feelings you have of stepping out on that field, but it's special. It's really special."

What Kosar appreciated most about that stadium, though, was not its atmosphere—it was that lousy, muddy turf, that infuriating, uncertain footing. Other players complained about the bad field slowing them, making them kind of downshift in their running, but that was never a problem for Kosar.

"See, I only have one gear," he says, laughing. It only slowed down the guys trying to catch him, which made his life a little easier. That famously slow run, that gawky stance, though, is something that never bothered Kosar. For one thing, when people said he looked like a fan out there, he would have been glad, sometimes, to give the fan a chance. "With all the hits I took, he could have taken my spot," he says, laughing again. "But my philosophy is, hey, it's a results-oriented world, a results-oriented game. It's not how you look: Just get it done."

A Cleveland attitude if there ever was one, and certainly Kosar got it done, so many times. "I remember the Jets game, the playoff games," he says. "I remember breaking the jinx in Three Rivers . . . I remember an overtime game in Cleveland we had to beat them. A lot of those Bengals games . . . I remember my first start down in the Houston Astrodome." A game, by the way, the Browns won, 21–6.

"And there are obviously some from the other end, too," Kosar goes on. As he speaks he has just returned from a brief vacation with none other than John Elway and his family, but that doesn't change certain things: "People won't ever let me forget about the Drive," he says. Has he developed perspective on that game? Win or lose, it was a football classic, a game fans will never forget. Does he look back and see it as kind of an honor just to have been involved in such a memorable contest?

"Maybe that will come with age," Kosar says, "But that hasn't happened with me yet. I didn't like to lose—I took losing hard."

Still, those tough Denver losses are some years behind him now, and Kosar has a pretty good feeling about what being a Brown has meant to him. "God has certainly blessed me," he says. "To have played 12 years, to play most of that career with my boyhood team, I've been blessed. I've received more than I thought I could get, and I think it's important to try to give something back." Part of that he does through his extensive charity work, mostly with kids, and part of it by responding to Browns fans. "It's a situation that is truly unique, and there aren't many areas and places that have this relationship between team and fans." He worked to help bring the new team to town, and he works with the team now, helping advise on the community marketing and charity sides of the game.

He'd like to be able to give more to the fans individually, he says, but the demands are almost impossible. "The fans are so nice," he says. "But the challenging thing now, you have three kids, you're married, you have lots of business and charity ventures going on, stuff that in itself would take your whole day. There's not enough hours in the day to do all the stuff going on." He lives in Florida, works all over the country. But his family is in Ohio, friends are in Ohio. Two weeks may go by that he's not in Cleveland, but four probably don't.

He doesn't stop, because he figures the teams, the players, still owe something to their towns. "I do think sports is at an interesting crossroads," he says. "I think everyone has to be cognizant of that. I really do think the strength of the NFL and the teams lies in that there's a bond between players and the community. I think it's essential that you have to try to maintain that."

And if they're looking for a model, he thinks he knows where they can start.

Browns Backers Everywhere

A Moment with Bob Grace and Jeff Wagner

IN THE ORIGIN MYTH of the Browns Backers—say it all together now: "the biggest professional sports fan club in the world" (as if anybody keeps statistics on such things)—Bob Grace started everything, but Jeff Wagner is the guy who turned it into something huge. Between the two of them they represent Browns fans at home and far off, Browns fans who make something happen.

In fact, according to Grace, that's exactly the point. The fans made this happen: "That's how I feel about the Browns Backers," Grace says. "The team didn't start this, the NFL didn't start this. The fans started this."

The Browns Backers started in Cleveland in 1984, when a group of Browns front-office types and some local fans sat down to come up with a plan for dealing with the volume of letters and phone calls coming in to the Browns office from fans looking for a deeper connection with their team. Browns director of operations Denny Lynch was aware of some small fan organizations in Seattle, which had in turn been modeled after the old Baltimore Colts Corrals. But the Seattle organizations were exclusively local, and the Colts Corrals—well, the Colts had just moved away from fans who had, at the end, stopped supporting the team. The Browns, on the other hand, had a fan base that was enormously solid at home, and growing stronger outside Cleveland every month, because of the decades of flight from the city. Lynch was looking to offer organization to Browns fans hither and yon, and he got together with some local fans, like Grace, a guy who owns a marine engineering company in Cleveland.

Grace was a lifelong fan—"my first conscious memory of rooting for the Browns was a playoff game, and I was painting the basement with my dad," he says. "I was eight or nine." He seemed to do more than just root for the Browns, though—he seemed to know them. "The players worked in the community and lived in the community." They were part of things. A couple, for example, were in an investment club with his dad. "Mike Lucci came into the house and shook my hand, I'll never forget it—it was a big hairy catcher's mitt."

His family had season tickets—had them since 1946. "If it wasn't my dad, it was one of my uncles." And he looks at the Browns, their fans, the city, that incredible bond, and he sees something that to him is very simple: "We've made this team. We've sold out the games year after year.

"Football started here. We were the ground floor. That's what makes us more important." It did start here—Canton is just down the road, Massillon, Ohio State. "Paul Brown, the whole history. Everything started right here and we were part of it."

He had even tried out for the Browns when they held an open tryout in 1978, after he left the marines. "That lasted all of about two hours," he says. He's a linebacker and there were a lot of linebackers on that team. Still, somehow, he ended up friends with some of the guys on the team, and with people in the front office.

When Lynch had the idea for starting "a fan club that didn't compete with the Touchdown Club but that was for the beer-and-bologna people," Grace was in the room, and he became the first president of Browns Backers Central, a sort of clearinghouse for Browns fans everywhere. "Every letter to the Browns office, local or out of town, expressing interest in the team, it was forwarded to me. I would send them a letter and a starter kit."

A lot of those letters came from locals, but an awful lot came from out of town. In fact, by the time 1995 rolled around, there were more than 200 Browns Backers clubs worldwide, and no other pro sports team could claim anything close to that. It turns out, Grace says, that there's just something special about being from Cleveland. "What's the ingredient that makes us special?" he asks. Part of it is that underdog thing. "I spent six years in the navy, and people would find out I was from Cleveland and I would get laughed at." He knew different, of course—"East Side, West Side, Slovenian, black, Italian, and we all live next to each other," he says. "This is the best. This is the melting pot." The fallout from the city's default years finally integrated the citizens, business, and politicians into a working whole, but Grace sees something simpler.

"You just had to be from Cleveland."

Another guy who believes this is Jeff Wagner, who in 1985 started one of the first of the far-flung Browns Backers clubs, in Southern California. Wagner's family had moved away from Cleveland in 1960, when he was 10, but he was Brown by then. "In 1964 we were visiting my aunt and uncle in Palm Beach. The family went out on a boat and I stayed home and watched the championship game."

He's never wavered. "Cleveland is just a working-class community," he says of the town he left. "Football was what bound people together during the winter. There's just great pride there. The fact that the Browns had such a wonderful tradition, it gave people something to say, 'This is ours, and we're something special.' Then came Bernie Kosar, the first player in sports to say, 'I want to play in this city.'"

Wagner ended up in Los Angeles in 1976, and for years he kept up with the Browns as best he could. Then he heard something about this Browns Backers business and contacted Grace. "I think there were three chapters when I called," he recalls. He wrote a letter to the editor of the forerunner of *Browns News Illustrated* announcing that he had wrangled a promise from a bar in L.A. to pull in the Browns on satellite one weekend.

"We got about eight of us," he recalls. When they got to the bar, though, they discovered that the bar couldn't get the game. "So we rushed over to the apartment of one of the guys, who called his friend in Cleveland." For a $45 phone call, they listened to the entire game over the phone.

"The ironic thing is it was a [speakerphone]" Wagner says—one of those where if you speak, you can't hear the person on the other end. "So every time someone would whisper, the sound would be cut off." So, miming reactions and engaging in silent high fives, they spent three hours around the phone.

"The next week," he says, "the game was on." The rest of the story is familiar: They got the *Cleveland* magazine subscriber list for their area, and were packing in 200 people by the end of their first year—by 1995 they commandeered 27 bars every Sunday, stretching from Santa Barbara to San Diego. They organized group outings to nearby games, sending so many thousands of Browns fans that it is said that when the Chargers missed a field goal at home against the Browns one year, the cheer was so loud that the linemen picked up the kicker in celebration, thinking it had been good. Wagner had to resort to a telephone play-by-play in 1993 during a Cincinnati game, but other than that, being the president of the largest Browns Backers group away from Cleveland is pretty much routine now.

So why, Jeff, why? Why the Browns and nobody else? Every sports bar in the country shows every game in the league, and you can always find a few guys in Giants shirts, a couple Packer fans, some Bills guys.

Browns fans, meanwhile, take up 27 bars from Santa Barbara to San Diego.

Why?

"There's a kind of camaraderie and pride in growing up in Cleveland," Wagner says. "It's a people city, not a glamour city. They're very down-to-earth people, and that's why they're unified."

So that's it. You keep asking why, and the answers never get much more complex than "Because." Clevelanders love their town, love their Browns. End of story.

So you ask one more time, and Jeff Wagner shrugs.

"There is no place," he says, "like Cleveland."

Things Change

THINGS CHANGE in January 1987, during that famous double-overtime game against the Jets.

For more than a decade the Browns have been a kind of troubled team. There was that one brilliant year in 1980, but beyond that they've been also-rans. A good year is 9–7, they don't make the playoffs; a bad year is when they're out of it by November. I know what it feels like to be a Browns fan—it feels like losing.

And then comes Kosar, and that 1985 playoff game, and then in 1986 the Browns go 12 and 4, rolling into the playoffs, and we all cover our secret doubts and act like we know it: This is going to be their year. In fact, they win home-field advantage throughout the postseason, and their first game is against the Jets. Living in Philadelphia, I go to a friend's house to watch the game, and in some ways I'm delirious—for example, the first highlight of the game is the first televised glimpse of that marvelous ancient, gray stadium filled with rocking fans: "Look!" I say. "That's my stadium! That's my town! Those are my guys! Look—it's the Browns!"

There's the stadium, there's the fans, and they look not like the bunch of ragtag losers I've grown up with but like one of those other teams—the Raiders, say, or the Dolphins. They look like fans and a team expecting a win. But underneath it all I'm still the product of those 1970s and 1980s Browns teams. "How sad," I think. "They're all going to be so disappointed."

And I'm right. The Browns play okay but nowhere near

their capacity, and the longer the game goes on the more it looks like the Browns have it in mind to lose. They sputter and miss, never quite finding their rhythm. The fans keep it up as best they can, but they're not rocking by the fourth quarter. When Freeman McNeil scores a touchdown late, the Browns are down by 10 with less than four minutes to go, and hope dies everywhere. It's getting kind of depressing in Cleveland, and I'm getting depressed in Philadelphia, but it's nothing I haven't seen before.

Then suddenly, yes it is—it is decidedly something I haven't seen before.

From nowhere the gods change their minds. Suddenly, with moments to go, the Browns are getting every call, plays that failed all day are suddenly working. They've got to move fast, and they do. It's like the 1981 Raiders game all over again, and the Browns are making it happen. They score a quick touchdown, they get the ball back, there's just—just!—enough time if everything goes right, and then comes an unforgettable play.

Kosar drops back to pass, heaves one the length of the field, and Webster Slaughter pulls it in at around the New York five. The clock is running and the Browns are out of time-outs, but they're on the five, and a field goal will tie the game—and they blow it.

Or almost—the thing is, I am *sure* they will blow it. When Slaughter gets up from his tackle at the five, he starts jumping around and celebrating. Many other players join him, and the Browns seem about to squander their last ticks of the clock on idiotic dancing and celebration, when all they have to do is line up, spike the ball, and then kick a field goal. But they won't—they're dancing, they're celebrating, the clock is ticking, even the announcers are pointing out the danger, and my stomach is churning.

And then Bernie Kosar makes his labored rush down the field, gets his teammates' attention, and spikes the ball. And then the Browns kick a field goal, and the game goes into overtime, but everything is already changed from that moment on.

I remember watching that premature celebration and thinking, "Oh, so *this* is how they blow it." I've been watching the Browns for my entire life, and have never seen them win a playoff game. I don't live in a world where that is possible. And then Kosar steps in, and I do.

My dad is there, and my sister is there, and later they tell me about it. "It was like part of the cheering was for ourselves, because we stayed, because we didn't give up," my sister says. My dad just says it's the most memorable game of his life—and don't forget, he watched Otto Graham play, and Jim Brown.

At the stadium and in front of televisions all over the country, Browns fans start watching the Browns in a new way. I watch the Browns take the ball early in the overtime and drive, and I think, "This must be what it feels like to root for the Dolphins, for the Raiders. This is what it's like to believe your guys are going to win." Maybe, I think, that Red Right 88 business is over with.

The Browns fail to score on that drive, the overtime drags on brutally, yet that certainty never dies. Up and down the field the teams slog, staggering, taking wilder and wilder swings, like two heavyweights struggling in the final rounds of a fight, each wishing someone—anyone—would fall. And finally it becomes clear: The Jets are tiring faster than the Browns. In the second overtime period the Browns get close and nudge a field goal through the uprights. The stadium erupts; Cleveland erupts.

I call my family at my aunt's house, where I hear them screaming over the phone. They think I am my mother's brother, Uncle Ronnie. In the madness, I cannot determine whether I am able to explain that I am not. My dad tells me later that after that game is his favorite moment as a Browns fan—under the lights, rocking the stadium, the fans decline to leave, just cheering the win, cheering Kosar and Newsome and Byner and Mack, Matthews and Golic and Hairston, cheering each other, cheering themselves. Years of belief and it's come to this, and they've won. It's a miracle, and he tells me over and over again: "Nobody wanted to leave," he says of the crowd seething and roaring under the lights in the cold late afternoon in Cleveland. "I mean, you just wanted to stay there and enjoy it."

Something has changed, all right. Now we all know we can win. Now we all expect to win next week, and we expect to go to the Super Bowl. Our days of bad luck are over, and now we're confident.

Bring on the Denver Broncos.

The Drive, the Fumble, and All That

DENVER.

You don't need to say another word to Browns fans, and an entire era comes into view. Heartbreak, unfairness, a team that peaked exactly at the same time as ours did only about a half a click better, a team that seemed to know how to beat the Browns, only the Browns, always the Browns.

What's funny, though, is it did not all start with the Drive. Oh no. It started sometime in the 1960s, when Art Modell supposedly opined that the Denver Broncos would play in Cleveland over his dead body. That was in the early days of the AFL, and the Broncos stood in for those AFL teams, still considered soft, considered suspect. Modell, perhaps forgetting that the Browns had themselves once come from another league considered suspect, derided the Broncos for the benefit of a wire reporter, or so recalled Dick Connor if the *Denver Post* in an October 1971 column. As the teams prepared for their first-ever Cleveland meeting, Connor's column made sure every fan would recall Modell's words.

I attended the game. The Broncos had Floyd Little; the Browns had Leroy Kelly. The Broncos had virtually no history; the Browns had one of the richest traditions in the NFL.

And after the game, the Broncos had 27, and the Browns had nothing.

That was the start. That was the first time the Browns hosted the Broncos, and things never got much better. The Browns may have feared doing damage to the only other team in the league that used orange in their uniforms, or it could have been some kind of karmic thing that I could never figure out. But the Browns never looked like they wanted to beat the Broncos, and even when they won it looked kind of accidental. At the time of their 1986 playoff game their record against the Broncos was three wins and eight losses.

There was no reason to think about that then, of course. Still, nervous, I tiptoed around the whole week leading up to that playoff game. *The Browns might be in the Super Bowl*—the thought would sneak up on me at odd hours. I'd be sweeping the house—*Super Bowl* would suddenly flash in my mind. I'd be working on a project, editing this or that—*If the Browns win* . . . and I'd daydream for half an hour. This was uncharted territory for me, and I stepped gingerly, testing the ground as if it were thin ice. Little did I know.

A friend came over to watch that 1986 game in my tiny building in Philadelphia, in my tiny apartment on my tiny black-and-white television.

The game was close; defensive, but not dry. Tied at 10 at the half, the Browns down by a field goal after three, it was anybody's game. Then the tying field goal and then, unforgettably, that pass—Kosar to Brennan, who went down on one hand, changing direction, faking his man so completely that he fell. After Brennan scored, the television kept showing that Denver defender sitting, shoulders slumped, at the end of his bench. He had lost the game.

The Browns had won. It seemed so clear. With the Broncos on their own 2-yard line and about five minutes to go, the

Browns had to make only one stop. My friend said as much. "I don't know," I said, not daring to say it: The Browns were going to the Super Bowl. I didn't say it, but I thought it—nervous and schizy, I ran up and down the hallway to the kitchen, play after play. I knew the game was theirs to win, but I had been to the Red Right 88 game—I didn't quite believe. Some part of me still said, "These are your Cleveland Browns—it's not in their karma to win."

Not hardly. The third-and-18 play, the barely missed sacks, the excruciating nearness of what was obviously going away, it all swelled up to fill the remaining minutes of the game, and when Elway completed his pass to Mark Jackson in the end zone, for me at least, it was only what even after the Jets game I had on some level feared would happen. The Browns won the overtime coin toss, but by then it was over. When the Browns had defeated the Jets a week before, their sneaking back into the game in the final minutes had broken the Jets' spirit. Just so now for us—it was only a matter of time, and the Broncos' winning field goal came mercifully quickly.

Still, that one wasn't so bad. It was exciting, it was heart-breaking, but the team was young. Things were just getting started. That one I got over pretty quickly.

The next year, though, I had found a friend, another Cleveland expatriate, who went to a Philadelphia bar called Bananas to watch the playoff games with me. Memory says her name may have been Ann. I still don't remember how we found one another, but we did, and we saw the Browns defeat the Colts in a playoff first-rounder, and we engaged in modest celebration. We didn't want to get our hopes up.

The January 17, 1988, AFC Championship against the Broncos found us sitting at the Bananas bar, where we were by then familiar to the extent that I knew the phone number and had given it to my sister in New York. The game started, and as often happens at unaffiliated bars, our screams and moans of dismay—the Browns, you recall, got in trouble early—motivated the opposition, and the bar seemed to take to the Broncos if only in distaste at our spectacle.

So the bar was happy. Seven nothing, 14 nothing, 21–3. The first half was ugly, ugly, ugly, and I recall laying my head on the bar in despair well before halftime. My sister called, from a bar in New York, and we urged one another to keep faith, though we didn't believe each other. Ann and I agreed that a blowout was at least easier to live with than the previous year's crushing last-minute disappointment, and we had a halftime beer in memoriam. Then the second half started, and the Browns quickly scored a touchdown. I remember at our cheers the bartender snidely asking, "What, the Browns get a first down?" I began to engage him in talk—21–10 is hardly an impossible margin, I was saying—but the Broncos scored again on a screen pass that somehow ended up going for a touchdown and as I recall the argument ended with my head back down on the bar.

The Browns were far from done, though. Kosar looked like the savior we wanted him to be and the entire Browns team looked like men on a mission. Bit by bit they came back, and we cheered almost viciously at the Broncos rooters in the bar. When the Browns tied it up at 31 the barkeep bought Ann and me each a beer. My sister called again, screaming into a phone in New York as I screamed into mine in Philadelphia, and we both promised each other to keep cheering and not to worry about what might happen.

Of course what might happen did, and quickly—the Broncos scored—and then to make it worse came that long drive, those agonizing hopes that the Browns might do to the Broncos exactly what the Broncos had done to the Browns the year before, in their home stadium, in front of their own fans. Then came that last play, with the Broncos line opening up like the Red Sea, with Earnest Byner spinning around and backing, almost effortlessly it seemed, into the end zone for the tying touchdown—and then, from nowhere, a hand, a swipe, the ball on the ground, the game lost and over. I interviewed David Modell once and he said that was his worst moment rooting for the Browns: "We were watching from the owner's box, and we knew he was going in, and then . . . dust. Dust."

Dust. The Broncos rooters howled in our faces, and Ann and I left the bar. I threw my hat across South Second Street, then picked it back up. This was Red Right 88 and the Drive all over again, and if the Jets game had briefly shaken my belief that the Cleveland Browns I rooted for had something karmatically unsprung, I was forever certain of it now. Ann and I bid a weary farewell out on the sleety Philadelphia street corner, and I made my way home, shoulders slumped.

There's the Drive, the Fumble, and the Blowout, people say, but they forget that in that third championship game against the Broncos, with Bernie Kosar's ailing right arm held together by what looked like coat hangers and rubber bands, the Browns fought to within 24–21 in the third quarter. The Broncos made quick work of them then, but still . . . there was a moment there. There was a moment.

But that was it, really. I remember in 1989 the Browns struggled to a 16–13 win over the Broncos during the season (ending a 10-game losing streak), and I remember a phone call from my brother trying, desperately it seemed to me, to find in that victory a change of fortune for the Browns.

I didn't think so, and I still don't. The Browns beat the Broncos the next year, 30–29, but the Browns were 3–13 that year, and if the highlight of your season is a one-point victory over the 5–11 Denver Broncos, you haven't had much of a season, and to be sure the Browns hadn't.

The funny thing about the Denver rivalry is that it just kind of ended. For those couple years, that late-eighties moment when the Browns were struggling to be the king of the AFC hill, the Broncos were rivals, and hated and feared as such. But when the Browns lost to the Broncos every year from 1991 through 1994 it was just another damned loss. Denver was no Pittsburgh, no Cincinnati even. The Broncos were a rivalry for a moment in time. As in the early Browns' rivalries with the Lions and the Giants, the Broncos were a great team, a tough team, a team that for a period seemed to have the Browns' number. But when the championship face-offs ended, so did the rivalry. There was a moment, but then they were just the team that beat us in all those miserable AFC Championship games. They were linked to the Browns for that period, and it's no surprise that they finally won their championships during the years when the Browns did not even exist. Perhaps they were using up too much of their juice just getting by the Browns, and with the Browns out of the way the Broncos had their shot in the Super Bowl, and they made good. Maybe in those years they purified their karma.

Let's hope the same happened to the Browns.

"Three disappointments"

A Moment with Ozzie Newsome

 OZZIE NEWSOME answers the question with no impatience: "People ask me 'what are your greatest memories of the Browns?' and I bring up three disappointments."

Yep—three. All three. Red Right 88. The Drive. The Fumble. All three games, there was Ozzie Newsome. When the Browns made their U-turn, from perennial winner to the league leaders in "almost," Ozzie was there for the experience.

"That's true," he says from his office at the Baltimore Ravens. "There's a lot of disappointment there. During the glory days in the fifties and sixties they were the flagship of the fleet. Then we became the bridesmaids. We could never get over that final hurdle."

Which hurt the most?

That's easy. "The first one," Newsome says. "That was our first shot at the playoffs, and just the way the game ended . . . We won in dramatic fashion, and we lost the same way. The way that game unfolded, everybody said, 'OK, here we go! Here's how it's gonna happen!' And then . . . we lost."

The Denver games were excruciating, but not like that. "The last two, putting ourselves in position to go to the Super Bowl but not being able to get there, that was hard." About the last Denver game Newsome says only, "That was the blowout."

Those losses were hard to take, but harder still for the connection he felt with those fans, he offers. Newsome played his college ball at Alabama, where the fans know something about support, about love. "We had some passionate fans," he says. "Fans who followed the University of Alabama football, fans who adored University of Alabama football. What I say to people is coming to Cleveland, especially what we endured in 1980, it surpasses even what I was used to with the University of Alabama."

Okay. Why?

Newsome brings up the usual points. "The city at that point was the butt of a lot of jokes around the country. Defaulting, the river burning, just a lot of negative things being joked about. All of a sudden we became a hot football team and people had something to be proud of Cleveland for.

"And we were a close team. We became a close team. It became one of those things, the expectation level of each individual in the huddle was, 'Now who's gonna do it this week?'"

That closeness extended beyond the huddle to the fans, of course. "Absolutely. I think it's a bond between the fans and the players within the community. It's not just something that happens on Sunday. It's something you live with 24 hours a day and seven days a week. The Browns game was played seven days a week, from one game to the next."

Did that kind of attention get on his nerves?

Just the opposite, Newsome says. "You appreciated that." The fans' love was reciprocated, and instead of dodging them he found a way to become part of them, part of their lives, part of their city. "You just started to frequent places . . . where you just became part of the fabric. 'This is where Ozzie hangs out.' It wasn't a hassle at all."

He had his own rituals—for example, taking a lap around the field before warm-ups—and the fans would become part of even those. "Certain fans would be there every game," he says. It was a good feeling to see them. "It was just, I'm ready, and you all are ready."

It was hard to get used to the idea that the Browns were actually leaving Cleveland—"You know how you're in denial? Probably for about a year and a half, I thought one day I was going to wake up and I was going to be back in Cleveland. I kept thinking, this is a dream."

But it wasn't. Ozzie Newsome works for the Ravens now, and from the front office he's making a contribution to Baltimore fans the way he did from the field for Cleveland fans— "This is how I feed my family. This is my team. My imprint is on this team." But he's looking forward to coming to Cleveland when the Ravens play the Browns. "It's going to be great to go in and compete. And I think they have a natural rivalry." Another rival—another series of great games, some unforgettable wins, and probably not a few more near misses.

Oh, yeah, Ozzie, speaking of which—Red Right 88. If the universe had been just a little kinder, if Mike Davis of the Raiders had been a little slower, if the ball had come close, . . . um . . .

"Oh, no question," Ozzie Newsome says. "I was gonna catch it. No reason to drop that one."

Autographed Picture

ONE EVENING, in Philadelphia, I attend a dinner party. I have to leave early to go to my job on a newspaper copy desk, and one of my wife's friends, a woman named Barbara, follows me out the door, abashed, almost skulking after me. She catches me on the porch, her head down, embarrassed.

"I have something for you," she says.

I'm delighted. What is it?

She pulls at her fingers, temporizing. "Well, I hope you don't think it's stupid," she says. "I mean, I don't know if you'd want it, or anything, but . . . well, I just kind of . . ." I narrow my eyes. "What is it?"

She looks me in the eye. "Well, my mother lives in Florida, and in her development there's a guy who used to play pro football, and . . . and I know you like sports, so . . . I hope you don't think it's stupid, but I got her to ask him to sign a picture for you."

"That's great," I say. I have a row of pictures along the wall in my office—buildings, athletes, other memorabilia from my different brushes with sports as a writer. Wonderful pen-and-ink drawings of stadiums by the sports artist Andy Jurinko; a photo of a professional lacrosse player in mid-pounce; an aerial shot taken in the 1920s during construction of Philadelphia's J.F.K. Stadium, which once held a hundred thousand people every year for the Army–Navy game. No autographed pictures, though—I've always resisted that. I enjoy meeting athletes or artists or other celebrities, enjoy meeting anyone who's reached the highest level at whatever they do. But I've always preferred a handshake to an autograph. What will you do with an autograph, after all? Unless it's someone who means enough to you to frame their picture and hang it up, it'll just end up in a drawer somewhere. With drawers full of postcards and ticket stubs already, an autograph, on a slip of paper or an eight-by-ten glossy, will just end up lost in the strata.

Not that I never tried, of course. I remember being five years old—this was in 1964—and my mother taking me, along with my brother, older by two years, across the big street in front of our house to see a football player I kept calling Frank Brian. My brother, frustrated nearly to insanity by this gaffe, growled the words, "No, *Ryan*," to me so often that I remember the refrain to this day. I also remember arriving in the men's store in the strip mall to find—what? This skinny man in a suit, sitting at a table? This was a football player?

Certainly not. My distress so great I cried, I could not be comforted by the picture of him with his arm upraised, his number 13 showing, ready to throw. The picture only made me more certain. Despite the lies of the grownups around me—and my brother's palpable excitement—this big man in the white uniform was not the same as the man at the table, I knew, and I was deeply disappointed. My sullenly accepted picture developed a fold, which progressed into a rip, and soon afterward the picture was lost.

Then once, in 1971, I ventured to the May Company men's department to see my favorite player, Leroy Kelly. Older and wiser—anyway, prepared for him to be in a suit—I even had a question ready for him: Did he ever get nervous before he had to carry the ball?

"No, just before the games," he laughed, scrawling his name across a publicity picture of himself, helmetless, in the Heisman position, stiff-arming an imaginary tackler as he cut across the field. That picture, though I recall it showing up in underwear drawers and junk boxes for several years thereafter, eventually disappeared as well. Not for me the prized collection of old programs, old football cards, pennants, photographs, ticket stubs, plastic helmets, that my brother carefully maintained.

So the picture for which Barbara begins shyly rummaging in her purse this cool Philadelphia evening will lack context.

But that, somehow, will make it even better, whoever it is. He'll be my only one—an autograph for the non–autograph seeker, a delightful curiosity. Some second-string guard who took a few snaps for the Cardinals in the sixties? Some Detroit Lion who returned two punts in 1973? Some Kansas City Chief who started out as a Dallas Texan and spent the productive years of his life fixing trucks? In a way, the more obscure the better. I'll have a story: "No, I never met him, never saw him play, never even heard of him. But my wife's friend Barbara got me this picture. How cool is that?" I'll ask.

Barbara supports that thought as she rummages in her purse. "My mom said he told her, 'He'll have never heard of me,'" she says. I reassure her: Whoever it is, I'm sure it will be wonderful. She finds a plain white business envelope, with my name on it. She hands it to me with a pained smile, even stepping back, as though I might see this picture and strike her, scoff at her for wasting time—hers, my own, even the time of this forgotten tight end who ought to be left to his pleasant obscurity. I open the flap of the envelope and take out the postcard: Three-and-a-half by five-and-a-half, black-and-white, it is old and almost brittle. A little information on the back, but it is too dim to read that. I turn to the picture, look instinctively at the signature.

"To Scott, Best Wishes, Otto Graham."

I actually gasp. My mouth falls open, and I start laughing. Barbara cringes. "Is it stupid?" she asks. "Was he really bad?"

Otto Graham: Ten years with the Browns. Ten title games in ten seasons. Pro Football Hall of Fame. Otto Graham.

I try to explain to her that she has no idea what she has done, that she has been the vector for a connection that beggars description. That she has brought me something that is impossible, that is perfect, that is better than anything could be. I want to tell her about my dad talking about Otto Graham, about him telling my brother and me that our debates over Bradshaw versus Montana were pointless, that Graham was the best there ever was. I want to explain about what the Browns have meant to me, about what it could mean to have a picture of Otto Graham fling itself at me out of my friend's purse in the middle of the evening under a streetlamp in Philadelphia, but I give up.

Instead, I just laugh, and I jump up and down under the streetlight in the middle of the street in the Philadelphia night. I clutch my picture of Otto Graham and jump around like I have just scored a touchdown, like I have lost my senses, like I have won the lottery. I jump with such joy that the door to the house opens and several of the party guests stream out the porch door to see what has happened.

"Otto Graham!" I shout. "Otto Graham! Barbara got me a picture of Otto Graham!"

A couple guys recognize the name, but for most he could be that second-string guard Barbara had feared he was. But he isn't some second-string guard. He's Otto Graham.

"That's wonderful," my wife says. "Now go to work." I do—and show my photo at the copy desk like a trophy. The copyeditors—almost universally, for some reason, deeply moved by sports—recognize the value of the connection, the inexplicable perfection of Otto Graham seemingly seeking me out like that. We read the back of the card—"College tailback, switched to T-quarterback in pros . . . Guided Browns to 10 division or league crowns in 10 years . . ." and on and on, ending with "Enshrined in 1965 in the Pro Football Hall of Fame in Canton, Ohio." Otto Graham.

And from nowhere he has reached out to me and sent me his picture, and I feel touched, I feel singled out, I feel anointed.

I feel Brown.

"No team will ever do that again"

A Moment with Otto Graham

I START OUT to explain to Otto Graham that his autographed picture sought me out by miraculous means, but I stumble and barely get out the first statement. "I'm from Cleveland," I tell him. "I grew up in Cleveland."

So he barks out a joke: "That's your problem!" he almost shouts, his chipper, cheerful voice ringing into the phone. Of course he doesn't remember signing that picture for me seven years ago, but he's perfectly glad to learn that he did so. Signing pictures is just part of his life, and if it makes people happy, so much the better.

"You enjoy it, most of the time," he says of the pictures or objects he receives to sign every day of the week. "My policy has been I will sign anything they send to me, and as long as I personalize it I won't charge anything at all." That is, as long as the photograph or pennant or football is for a fan, makes a genuine moment of connection between Graham and someone else, he's glad to do it. If it's somebody sending half a dozen photos and asking specifically for them not to be personalized—obviously to be sold to collectors at shows—Graham's not interested.

That connection with the fans, though, is more a by-product for Graham than for later generations of Browns players.

Players who came after him had a history: "You know, the parents saw us win a lot and they talked about the Browns to their kids," he says. "It just gets handed down from father to son to grandson. If you heard about the Browns all your life growing up, then you want to see 'em.

"Yeah," he says, "I think the Browns probably have overall about the best fans in the country," but for his generation it wasn't about tradition. For his generation, at least, the reason is obvious.

"Way back when we first started off, we won a lot. That creates fans. If you go out there and lose three quarters of your ballgames, nobody wants to see you. The fans were loyal because we won. People like a winner." Simple as that. "That's true in all walks of life. You're not going to go to a movie if the reports are bad on it."

Graham is proud of those early Browns teams. "We won 113, we lost 20, tied 4," he says of his 10 years with the Browns. "No team will ever do that again, because the competition is greater now."

And because no team has Paul Brown. "He revolutionized pro football," Graham says. "In fact, Vince Lombardi came to our camp a few times. I learned a lot about life from Paul Brown, I tell you that. He doesn't get credit like a guy like Lombardi gets, but Paul Brown did more to revolutionize pro football than anybody."

Graham often looks back at his decision to play for the Browns in the AAFC instead of the Lions in the better-established NFL as one of the best of his life. The Lions had drafted him and not bothered to send him a contract, but in 1945 Paul Brown came to where Graham was stationed in the Navy Air Corps and offered him a contract as well as a monthly stipend until the end of the war. Graham signed the contract. The Lions got wind of the deal and called him to see about breaking it. "I said what the hell do you mean, break it?" Graham says. "I signed it in good faith, I'm gonna honor it."

He chuckles for a moment. "I sure made the right choice. Not that I was brilliant—I was lucky. I just made a good guess. It's amazing how things went back then." Graham says he's lucky not only that the Browns' tradition became something special. He's lucky, he says, because if he hadn't played for Brown, "I would have been nowhere near as good as I turned out to be." Of Brown's famous regimented approach, he says, "We beat them through organization. For 10 years I brought out those playbooks. Rehearse rehearse rehearse, practice practice practice. We didn't enjoy it, but we had to do it. He just made us think football all the time."

Well, maybe Graham was a little more than lucky: "I'll make you a bet I'm the only guy who made All-America in football and basketball in the same year [at Northwestern] and then played professional basketball and professional football." Pro basketball? Yep. In the 1945–46 season, after he was out of the service but before he started playing for the Browns, Graham had some time to kill so he played one season for the Rochester Royals in the old National Basketball League, forerunner of today's NBA. In the process he won one more championship trophy than Charles Barkley, Karl Malone, and Shaquille O'Neal combined.

Graham learned about business and life from Paul Brown, not just football. "As I look back on it, our very first year he fired our captain, Jim Daniell, because he had been arrested for drunken driving." Daniell was the center on the 1946 team, and he got into a scuffle with the police. The next day in practice, Brown asked if what he had heard was true. Daniell said it was. "Everybody was deadly quiet," Graham recalls. "Then Brown said, 'Turn in your suit. You're through.' It happened just like that. If you don't think he got our attention . . ."

119

Graham later recognized something else: "His replacement was just as good as Jim, so we didn't hurt the team." In that Graham sees lessons about how to run a business, how to be a leader, how to be part of a team. Graham says in another walk of life Brown would have been an admiral or CEO—Brown had found a way to enforce his rules about behavior without hurting the team. "Everything was for the welfare of the team, the business we were in. I mean, if Otto Graham's out getting drunk, that's the Cleveland Browns getting drunk."

As one of the very first Browns, Graham sees Browns fans through less rosy lenses than many. "You talk about fans, they were great," he says, "but [in later years] there were a bunch of guys in the end zone—it was the Dawg Pound years later. I read about this. People would throw objects, like flashlight batteries. You can hit a player in the eye and blind him. That kind of stuff went on. The Dawg Pound got laughs and favorable press, but that's terrible. That's a disgrace. If it had been me, I'd have the police there every week."

He'd stop all alcohol sales, too—"You get doctors, lawyers, they get half drunk, they become animals. I would never allow them to serve any liquor. Not even beer."

No alcohol . . . responsive but polite fans . . . free autographs . . . plenty of practice . . . deep personal modesty . . . a broad general decency. This is a guy whose team I'd play on. This is a guy I'd root for.

I want this guy's autograph.

Rumors of War and the Last Pittsburgh Game

To BROWNS FANS it's like the moment you heard about the space shuttle or John Lennon or John F. Kennedy. All Browns fans remember the moment in 1995 when they first heard that the team was leaving town. I pay attention to the Browns, but I kind of missed the call on this one.

I'm sitting at my desk at the newspaper where I work in North Carolina, and someone shouts across the newsroom— "Hey, Huley, what do you think about Baltimore?" Confused, I wonder if he's asking whether I know a good place to stay—is he planning a visit?

No, he explains—the wires are full of stories about a possible Browns move to Baltimore.

I roll my eyes, expel breath dismissively. "Nope. No way. Never happen." The Browns will never leave Cleveland, I explain, launching into an arrogant explanation of economics and fan support and franchise lore. Absolutely never happen, I keep saying, day after day, until one day everyone gathers around a television set and watches a news conference explaining that the Cleveland Browns are moving to Baltimore.

I hear about the rest of it through my dad, through my brother, through news stories. From ugly rumor to dispiriting reality so quickly I barely have time to register the events.

I want to turn away in disgust—I want to take this as my final opportunity not to care. In recent years the Browns have disappointed far more often than they've delighted; they're a political trouble spot in Cleveland, their coach and owner seem to have no friends among fans or civic leaders, their play is distressing.

Add to that some changes in my own life and the way I see football.

For one thing, insane fitness regimens and steroid use have turned football players, always big and sometimes giants, into something truly weird: 300-pound behemoths who fling one another around, snapping bones like they're twigs. Maybe I've seen the tape of the Joe Theismann injury one too many times, and that stuff just starts to look ugly. Add the in-your-face antics of everyone from Deion Sanders to Webster Slaughter that have turned football—like all sports—from a game of "I win" into a game of "you lose," and that's even uglier. I'm sick of commercials slowing down games, of players changing teams year by year. I'm starting to lose my spirit.

In fact, in 1994, the Browns had made the playoffs at about the time that my wife was leaving me, and I sat at the house of a friend watching the playoff game against Pittsburgh a week after she'd moved out. The game, naturally enough, didn't register much—more, though, it was hard not to feel a little bit pathetic. What I had hoped would be sustaining and energizing—"You're life's in a bit of a slump, but there's always the Browns, buddy!"—felt more like an exercise in wasted time. All this madness going on in my own life and I was sitting in front of the television, watching a football game?

So my first reaction, from my North Carolina home, to the Browns' move, is an earnest sigh of relief. I'll get my life back, my Sundays back. Good riddance to the whole thing. Modell, the politicians, the coach, the players, throw them all in the same bus and send them to Baltimore. I can't care anymore.

Then my brother calls. Then my dad calls. And before I know it I'm scheduled to go see the Browns play, for the last time, against Pittsburgh no less, in late November. And before I know it I'm looking forward to it.

In front of the stadium that day, a lot of people want my attention. Someone wants me to sign a petition in favor of riverboat gambling, which would generate revenues to improve the crumbling stadium enough to attract another team. Someone else gives me a photocopied sheet with a message from Mayor Michael White urging me to behave—angry or not, Browns fans are going to be on national television. Someone else has a circular about seizing the team through eminent domain—he's from the Ohio Communist Party.

We troop over the West Third Street Bridge and we stand out there, my brother, my sister, and I, and we watch the circus. We comment on the switch—Pittsburgh tickets are being all but given away on the day of the game; meanwhile, tickets for an Indians season still four months distant went on sale two days previously, and 200,000 tickets went on the first day.

Then we go in. We talk a little about history—who was at the game where Bradshaw got hurt, who was at the game where Greene kicked McKay, who saw the collapse against Denver, the win against Dallas. We wonder whether Baltimore people will care about such things.

There are 67,000 people making memories instead of watching the game, which never quite gets our attention, especially after the Browns stumble out of the blocks. We barely notice when the Browns finish the first half with a touchdown to cut the deficit to seven.

I take a walk around the concourse, listening to the echoing grumbles, and the second half starts while I'm on my journey. I'm pleased to notice that when the Browns start moving I can't be bothered to rush to my seat—I just hustle out of one of the portals and watch right there from the aisle.

And from there I realize that Cleveland Stadium is—for a moment—the same place where I grew up. When the Browns line up near the goal line and the crowd's roar echoes through the great horseshoe, for that moment I believe. Maybe a court case can make the Browns—and the NFL, and Big Sports everywhere—stop and reconsider their place in the world, reconsider the point of city-based teams in the first place.

And when Vinny Testaverde hustles around right end and dives into the end zone, and when it appears the Browns might win, I give the day's only true shout of joy, and I get back to my seat with my brother and sister. My dad's there too, visiting from his regular seats.

That the Browns kick away the game after that is only one last disappointment for a group used to disappointment.

I don't know then whether the Browns will ever be back—relocated team, expansion team, court battle, team colors, it's all rumors now. And I'd like to let go of the whole stinking mess.

But I can't.

Because what I remember most that day is not Vinny's touchdown but something that occurred in front of that grimy, yellow-brick stadium before the game. Taking my eyes off the picketers and pamphleteers and the anger and the disgust, I had turned to the West Third Street Bridge.

Beyond the bridge I could see the sawteeth of drawbridges on the Cuyahoga River poking into the low blanket of late-afternoon clouds. I could see the city of Cleveland, new and bright but as Brown as ever, glittering behind it.

On the bridge I saw only fans. Under the steel-gray sky, thousands upon thousands, wearing orange and brown and coming to watch a football game. It was the last mustering, and here they came. They came in a constant flow, over the same bridge I had crossed with my dad for parts of four decades. Fathers and sons, husbands and wives, friends and rivals, swarming over the bridge to the stadium. They had orange hats, silly jerseys, masks, paint, and signs, but they were there. They were Browns fans, it was game day, and they were there.

For what it was worth, so was I.

Big Dawg and the Man in the Brown Suit

 By now he's become a celebrity—in fact, almost a cliché. John "Big Dawg" Thompson, the great big guy in the dog mask and the orange construction helmet, woofing in the end-zone bleachers. Any time an NFL broadcast originated from Cleveland after 1985, you saw that shot sometime during the show.

Then it got to be more—John was adopted as a kind of civic symbol during the Save Our Browns movement. He's appeared at hundreds of functions, lunches, golf outings. He was honored at sporting events and banquets. He became a sort of mascot.

But that's nothing new for the Browns. The Browns have adopted fan mascots before—in fact, they may have invented the practice. Long before the guys with the pig noses rooted for the Redskins' line, long before Franco's Italian Army cheered Franco Harris and Gerela's Gorillas rooted for Roy Gerela, long before the Dallas Cowgirls cheerleaders, came the man in the brown suit.

Abe Abraham had been a friend of original Browns owner Mickey McBride. He helped out at the pass gate for that first season in 1946. Then during one game while walking around the closed end of the stadium, he got knocked over by a Lou

Groza field goal. That will wake a guy up, and before long Abraham was catching field goals and extra points in the broad open area behind the goal posts in the closed end of the stadium. One thing led to another and he ended up in a special gaudy brown suit, recognizable to all. Think of it—a guy who just kind of ends up friends with the team, playing along and becoming part of the show in an easy, informal way. It was a very Browns kind of interaction.

Abraham was actually the first celebrity I ever approached. One day at a Browns game he found himself for some reason in the upper deck near my dad's seats, and my dad pointed him out to me. "You know who that is?" he asked. He called him Mr. Brown. "That's the guy who catches the kicks! Why don't you go shake his hand?"

I did that, creeping towards him and asking: "Are you the guy who catches the kicks?"

"Yes," he said, smiling down at me and grasping my hand.

"Oh," I said. "Um, thank you." At a loss for anything further to say, I returned to my seat.

John Thompson, it turns out, was similarly awed by Abraham. "He was like an icon for somebody like me," he recalls, of his own days going to the Browns games as a boy, and of the days when Thompson, like Abraham, worked at the airport. "The man with the brown suit with his bald head and his glasses," Thompson says. "He was a classic."

And now, of course, it's Thompson who's a classic. "When you're a Browns fan, you're always thinking of something different to do," he says in the comfortable living room of his Cleveland home. "In 1980 I wore an outfit to the games—a papier-mâché head and the Browns flag." The head was in the shape of the elf, the little brownie that the Browns used as a logo way back when. "Abe was kind of the reason I did the crazy things I did."

And, like Abraham, Thompson turns out not to be cliché, not part of the marketing machine. His house looks like yours or mine—pictures of his kids, a big-screen TV where sports run in the evenings while he keeps half an eye on the kids out on the lawn, a tidy kitchen. A couple Browns things—a clock in the shape of a helmet, a sticker on the computer. And oh yeah—that dog mask and the helmet atop a bookcase. But that's it. Thompson may be Big Dawg and he may have his picture on the cover of *Sports Illustrated*, but he's a great big Browns fan is what he is.

He started out, like a lot of Cleveland kids, sneaking into the stadium for games. "We'd scale the TV cables up against the wall and climb in the bathroom windows," he recalls. Guards would see them, but by the time they arrived he and his friends would have scattered into the crowd. That all changed as his girth increased, though: "One year I couldn't fit in," he laughs. Stuck in the window, he saw the police gathering below him, and after trying to pull him through his friends gave up, finally pushing him back out the window. "It was so over," Thompson says. He got chased from the stadium that time and started buying his way in.

By 1980 he watched Red Right 88 from his season tickets in boxes in the closed end of the stadium, but when he got married in 1984 he had to add a seat for the '85 season, so he went to seat day at the stadium, where the seats available for season tickets were marked and season-ticket buyers could improve their station if they chose. "I had never sat in the bleachers before," he said, but he saw some open seats in the front row and walked over to check them out. "And then I take a walk down that ramp, and it's like you're walking out onto the field." John Thompson was home.

That summer during training camp, of course, Don Rogers and Frank Minniefield and Hanford Dixon started barking at their teammates in practice. "Then they were barking at receivers," Thompson says of the practices he attended. "Then they were barking at everybody." The fans picked up on it, and the barking started in the bleachers, and it's never stopped. The Saturday before the first game Thompson and his friends watched a college game at a bar. They were parked by a costume shop that had just opened up.

"After we were in the bar all day—feeling no pain—we walked into the shop." Up on the top shelf Thompson saw this homely dog mask. The clerk said it was 12 bucks but because the store was just opening—and because the mask was so awful—Thompson could have it for 10. "So I threw 10 dollars on the counter and said it's mine." Over the objections of his new wife and his buddies he started wearing it to games, and others followed suit. He remembers a doghouse brought into the stands that usually had a keg of beer in it. He remembers somebody who had painted a real dog skull brown and orange. He remembers all the guys in masks, in suits, with signs. Soon people were selling little barking-dog puppets, headbands with floppy ears. The bleachers—where my dad watched the 1964 championship game—had become the Dawg Pound.

"I first got asked for an autograph in 1986," he says. And after countless shots on television and interviews by reporters from every paper and station known to man, John Thompson wasn't just a big Browns fan—he was part of the show. "The biggest moment for me came in the Jets game," he says of the double-overtime win in 1986. He believes that the constant heckling of the Dawg Pound is part of what drove Mark Gastineau to commit his perplexing late hit on Bernie Kosar in that game, keeping a drive alive and helping the Browns win. "We really were a part of the game," he says. "It would have never happened if not for the Dawg Pound."

Thompson was a big part of the Save Our Browns effort, appearing at rallies, working with Mayor White and the city of Cleveland, and testifying in Congress. Yet despite the exposure—even overexposure—of the Dawg Pound, Thompson feels that the Dawgs are just another great example of the Browns' historically great fans. He points out that the Dawgs got their start completely independently, with no help from the league or the teams; that the players responded to the Dawgs emotionally; and that when the new stadium was built, in recognition of their loyalty, it included a special section in which no seat licenses were required. "When I testified in Congress, I said the Dawg Pound was created by the fans, and that they had profited from that over those 10 years," he notes.

Then he makes his central point: The team was welcome to profit from that, he says. Yeah, in a bottom-line analysis, the Browns had something to sell, and the fans bought it. "But they sold it to us personally," he says, simply. And it was that personal connection we all were glad to be part of, glad to buy tickets for. "I don't care if they made money, and made it off me," Thompson says. "It was something I wanted."

"Hundreds and hundreds of people openly weeping"

The Last Home Game

Since it was against the Bengals, the last game the original Cleveland Browns played at home—the last game played in Cleveland Municipal Stadium—was played in front of Paul Brown's family, and there's something satisfying about that.

What is startling is that the game seems to have offered so much satisfaction in other ways as well.

My dad was there. He couldn't visit his kids like he did during the Pittsburgh game three weeks before, because we weren't there. He went with his buddy like any other game, and what struck him was that the crowd at first didn't feel enraged—it didn't feel hopeful, it didn't feel lost. In fact, it didn't quite feel like a crowd at all, he says. "I think everyone was just so engrossed in themselves that this is the last game the Browns are playing, that we didn't feel together."

John "Big Dawg" Thompson saw it a little differently, sizing it up the way so many others did: he felt like he was attending a funeral. When he learned in November the team was moving, he says it was "like finding out that your best friend had a terminal illness and that he had eight weeks to live and you could see him four more times." He says he—and the other fans—went through stages of grief like anyone else.

The first game was about anger: "How the hell could this happen?" he asked. "I protested. I didn't wear my mask." The Browns were blown out by Houston. The next game was more about connection. "How can I bring it across to my friend that I'm with him?" he says he wondered before watching the Browns lose to Green Bay.

At that Pittsburgh game, Thompson says, I wasn't the only one who felt like I was at the last mustering of the Browns fans. "This is almost it," Thompson says fans felt, "and I'm gonna give it all I got."

Then the last game. "Coming back for the last game—you didn't even want to go," he recalls. "I was almost scared." He spoke at a protest before the game. He walked with a gang of fans—and reporters—to the stadium. He skipped his usual pregame cigar club with other Dawg Pound members.

In the pound, things were quiet. "There was no getting on opposing players," he says. "I mean geez—usually, if this was the Bengals . . ." He trails off. "There was none of that going on."

The game started, he says, "and I didn't know what to do. Then the players came out and started busting their ass, and then you knew. Hey—this game . . . we have to win!" It looked to Thompson like the players were trying to win one for the fans. A team that was 4–9 came out to lay a whupping on their intrastate rivals. "We all got into it, then," Thompson says. "We were cheering like nothing was even happening.

"And then about the last four minutes of the game, it all fell apart inside me."

What started it, he says, was the sound: "I started hearing the wood chopping all around me," as fans started ripping out their seats, either as souvenirs or in protest. Like the unbearably sad last echo of the roar that greeted the Browns to start each game, the clanking and sawing provided the final sound—the death rattle—of the Browns and their stadium. "I said, oh my God, it's over," Thompson recalls. "They played so well, but it's like your best friend is dying. They were winning the battle, but not the war. I thought the emptiest feeling was 1980, Red Right 88." But no. This was worse.

John Telich, news anchor at WJW-Fox 8 television in Cleveland, has covered the Browns since 1980, and he knew he was seeing something uncanny. "It's something unlike I've ever experienced before," he says. "I was a kid of 11 in 1964, and it's hard to describe the emotional attachment." On the field were former Browns from every era. "You remember seeing Jimmy Brown, Leroy Kelly, Greg Pruitt," he says of watching the Browns on the field over the years. "Then you look 10 feet away and you see Jim Houston, Brian Brennan. They came back for the funeral. It was like an open invitation to a funeral, and that's where they were on December 17, 1995. That's why it was absolutely bizarre."

He, too, says his most powerful memory from that game was of those seats being removed. "I remember the absolutely eerie sensation of hearing the seats being hacked away by the fans." Row after row of those seats came down, ending up in piles on the field.

The exact same thought comes from my dad—"They would unbolt an entire row," my dad says. "They would unbolt a row of three, four, five, ten seats, and pick them up, and pass them row over row onto the field, and when they got to the end they would dump them on the field. I thought it was great. It made me feel good. Here's the fans showing their contempt for Modell, but doing it in a nondangerous way. It was a happening. It was something you wanted to be there for. At that point we didn't even know if we were going to keep the colors, the name, we didn't know anything at that point. It was the last Browns game."

My dad took a piece of his seat with him. Thompson took something else.

"All of a sudden the game ended," he says. "I could see Earnest Byner take off for the stands, and a couple people coming out towards the Dawg Pound. People were crying, and I took off my mask." He saw Tony Jones running towards him, bringing a ball, which he threw towards Thompson. "I threw people off me to get that ball," Thompson laughs. He's still got it, and Jones has since signed it: "Keep up the fight, Big Dawg." Says Thompson, "That's going to stay in my family forever."

Telich, covering the game for television, was running around the field and he saw close up what those who were there will never forget and those of us who have seen it only on tape can barely grasp. "I took a lap around the whole stadium with Earnest Byner," Telich says. "I have never seen anything like the emotional attachment there.

"Hundreds and hundreds of people openly weeping. A lot of players were just absolutely overcome by emotion that day." Sportscasters too, Telich says. During a special on which he was working afterwards the crew kept having to break so the on-camera guys could get control of their emotions. "I got a call the next morning, one of the producers for CNN sports called. He said, 'Man, I was getting choked up just watching you guys.' It was just unbelievable."

Byner took that lap, from the Dawg Pound all the way back to the dugout, just touching and being touched, sharing a last redemptive moment with the fans who had loved him, cheered for him, agonized with him, forgiven him. Then he found the entry to that dugout and, fans clinging to his jersey, went into the locker room. Some players came back out for a while, but that was it. The tears, the sadness, the Browns. The end of something.

"We saw that," my dad says, and he and his friend took the only course of action left them.

"When most of them had gone in," my dad tells me, "we left."

"It was just a spirit thing"

A Moment with Earnest Byner

TWO THINGS HAPPENED on December 17, 1995. One was the Cleveland Browns played their last game at Cleveland Municipal Stadium, tearfully ending an era. The other thing—*mirabile dictu*—was that the Fumble became the second thing for which Browns fans would remember Earnest Byner.

The first would forevermore be the last lap. When the gun sounded on that final heartbreak in an era of heartbreaks for the Cleveland Browns, Earnest Byner didn't run for the locker room—he ran for the fans.

It wasn't something he planned. "It was just a spirit thing," he says now, from his office with the Baltimore Ravens. "It was something that just came about. It was appreciation, because the fans had been so good to me throughout my years in Cleveland."

Think about that just for a second. Just like Brian Sipe's standing ovation in that restaurant the day after Red Right 88, Earnest Byner found tremendous support after the fumble that dashed so many hopes in January 1988. "It seemed like the relationship they had was like a family member, almost," he says. "Thirty-, forty-year season-ticket holders. Sometimes you got negative things because of that, but no question, they were supportive throughout."

Still, after the 1988 season Byner had left the Browns for Washington, where he ended up scoring a touchdown in a winning Super Bowl XXVI effort. Karma being what it is, if Cleveland was going to suffer the heartbreak of losing the Browns, someone was going to have to soothe its feelings, and who better to do so than the man whose feelings the fans had soothed in 1988? Byner was back with the Browns starting in 1994.

"It was eerie," he says of returning to the team with whose fate he had been so closely tied. "I was more in tune with the spirit that goes with life and goes with the game then, more cognizant of my surroundings." So after all the interviews, the practices, he experienced a profound sense of recognition when he came back out in front of the fans for the first time. "Going out on that field and turning around, and seeing those Browns helmets, that was eerie." After a hiatus, an exile, he was Brown again, and the connections seemed to fill the stadium. "It was almost like a haze in the air," he says.

A good haze, though. Fans had forgiven that memorable fumble, and, more than that, accepted him, clutched him back almost as a symbol of their own suffering, claimed him as one of their own. "It was because of how I played the game," Byner says of his work ethic and every-down mentality. "With the Cleveland fans, if you got their approval, you had made it. Blue-collar, hard-nosed, if you gave it all you got, regardless of circumstances."

Byner says it simply: "If you found approval with Cleveland Browns fans, then you were a football player. You became a football player by getting their approval."

There's no record of a personal ad saying "Earnest—Please come back, all is forgiven," but when Byner returned he was welcomed by fans with open arms. And Byner was glad to be back—glad to be back where football meant not just something but everything. "I can tell you this," he says, recalling the Browns' 1985–1989 teams, "I've never felt that energy encompass a whole city like it encompassed Cleveland. A lot of the time I didn't want to go out of the house, because I got physically charged up by the energy that was around. I wanted to save that for the game. All those weeks and days were filled with just charged energy. Because, again . . . the fans." Not even in Washington, with a Super Bowl champion, did Byner feel that kind of energy. He was glad to be back.

And then, in 1995, the news. The Browns were leaving.

For a while after the announcement the players had a hard time focusing on football—they had houses to sell, lives to uproot, moves to consider. The team, struggling with a 4–5 record, went south completely after the formal announcement, losing five more in a row. "But the most difficult part was dealing with the fans," Byner says. "After one game, I remember this lady, a young blond lady, about my height, after one game she just boo-hooed on my shoulder. What do you do? How do you handle that situation?"

And then that final game at home, against the Bengals.

Byner says the team didn't have any win-one-for-the-fans speeches, but nobody ever had to get Earnest Byner up for a game—and Earnest Byner was playing his last game in front of the Cleveland fans who had treated him like a member of their family. Leroy Hoard had been hurt, and as the Browns put a hurting on the Bengals, Earnest Byner was chief assassin.

"I ran like I was a rookie," Byner says now. "Breaking tackles, running over people, four or five catches at least, over 120 yards rushing. I had a huge game. It was almost eerie to be a part of that whole situation again.

"It was so strange. It was almost like it was just meant for me to have that game."

And then the clock started winding down. "The seats were coming out of the stands, as we know—that was the start of the demolition of Cleveland Stadium," he says. "I was sitting on the sidelines next to Tony Jones, and we were just looking at the Dawg Pound. As soon as the clock ran down, we just took off.

"It was a lot of mixed emotions going on," he says, still wondering at the outpouring. "Some were just plain football fans, happy we had won the game. But you'd see people happy we were over there, but they had tears in their eyes. You almost had to pull them out of the stands to get them to let go.

"I was feeling some of their pain, and some of their happiness. You looked at those faces and you saw anger." He stops. "You know, I don't remember what I was thinking at the time. After going around that stadium, those thoughts were more towards the fans" than towards his own concerns. "I went to the Dawg Pound and lapped around to our dugout."

Then he went inside, and the next time he comes back he'll be a member of the Baltimore Ravens staff, which causes a smile. "If there ever was a rivalry that needed to be built up, this isn't the one." No, this one will take care of itself. But building up the Ravens' relationship with their fans is part of Byner's job now, and he knows it'll take a while. Every team develops a special relationship with its fans, some stronger, some less strong, as he saw in Washington.

But one thing he'll never forget, he says.

"It was different in Cleveland."

Two Friends from Denver

WHY DO WE LOVE FOOTBALL? Why do we love this ridiculous game?

One reason is because it has a result, a simple result. Our guys got the ball on the 30, with a minute left, down by four. Did they get the job done? Did they not? Why? Who dropped the ball, and who caught it? It was third-and-eight, and one fellow threw the ball and somebody else ran underneath and then we all cheered or we all groaned, and there you are. We can see it on the replay and we know what happened. Missed block? Dropped pass? Great catch? Rules infraction? It's all there. It takes place in the open, and stuff either happens or it doesn't and then you go home.

In our own lives we have too little of that. Take the Cleveland Browns and the complicated matter of their return to the NFL, under new ownership, wearing the same colors as ever after their three-year hiatus. If you want to figure out exactly how the team came back, you have to start weighing sources claiming varying degrees of credit and blame, and before long you're a lost spirit and disgusted with the whole thing. You've got the city of Cleveland, where a host of people would like to claim that they fought hard to keep those colors in town, and could have kept the team in town through court action if necessary. You've got people certain that Art Modell would have gladly given up the colors and history in order to get moving and that anybody who claims to have wrested them from him is a grandstanding fake.

Certainly the Browns Backers and Save Our Browns, with

their millions of petition signatures and their untold e-mails and faxes to the NFL and individual team offices, had an effect, though just how much it's hard to say. Browns fans and Browns Backers clubs going to other stadiums, to NFL owners' meetings—these had an effect, but nobody can gauge it. The machinations leading to the award of an expansion team, the behind-the-scenes deal-cutting, the decision to go with the Lerner ownership group rather than with any others, the stadium financing—all of these live in a gray area, a depressing, foggy place that is the opposite of sports. Who promised what to whom, what happened and when, nobody will say, perhaps nobody can say. We yearn for that third-and-eight clarity, we yearn for clear results.

We yearn for football.

Still, in 1996, disgusted at the beginning of the three-year hiatus, I tried not to yearn for football. It even worked for a while—a year, I guess. But then a funny thing happened.

I live in North Carolina now, and I've already got a lifelong friend from Pittsburgh. So the universe being the trickster that it is, it was odds on that when I moved here I'd make a lifelong friend from Denver, and that's how it happened, only it happened twice and I ended up with David and Joe, two guys with strong Denver ties. They good-naturedly went to my Browns Backers bar with me in 1993 and 1994 to watch the Browns play the Broncos, and they were highly decent about the Bronco victories both times. And then in 1997, while I was trying to ignore the NFL, my friends started getting heated up as their beloved Broncos got ready, they were sure, to disappoint them in the Super Bowl again.

Which is why none of us was quite prepared for it when we found ourselves, on January 25, 1998, circled in front of David's television set, standing, not quite believing, as something remarkable was about to happen for David and Joe.

David remembers the 1977 season, when the Broncos went to the Super Bowl for the first time. "It was just magic," he says, recounting a trip to the hardware store during a televised game. "In Denver, during the game, it's on TV and radio like background noise. I listened in the car, then I'm in the hardware store, picking up some PVC pipe, and Bernard Jackson intercepted a pass and returned it for a touchdown.

"People were literally dancing in the aisles in the hardware store, and I was right there with them. It was such a goofy memory of people going apeshit in the hardware store in the University Hills Mall."

So Denver or whomever he roots for, how can you not love this guy?

Of course Denver lost that 1977 Super Bowl, and several subsequently, as you may have heard. Yet there we were in front of the TV in 1998. All our years of rooting for our different teams, all our shared memories of this or that disappointment, and suddenly it looked like David and Joe were going to get their moment. David has snorted to me about the belief that a Denver victory would be a life-changing experience. He remembers a columnist before one of the Denver Super Bowl losses, predicting a win and writing, "We're about to enter the time of our lives." David is a guy who associates "the time of our lives" with things like world peace or the eradication of disease, so he rolled his eyes. Still, when John Elway helicoptered for that first down and then leapt up with that look in his eyes, David and Joe went to a Different Place, and it gave me goose bumps to see it. "That was the moment I thought, 'This really could happen,'" David recalls. Terrell Davis scored that touchdown, and then, miraculously, it looked like the Broncos would hold—and they did, and the clock ticked down.

"It took a millisecond," David says. "It was like, 'This

game's over! We just won the Super Bowl!' It was that extra millisecond of still waiting for the piano to fall on your head. Maybe 49ers fans get real blasé about it, but not me. You just can't believe it's really happening, that you're actually going to get the chance to run around with your finger in the air and go 'We're Number One!'"

Then a pause—and the down side. "On one hand it's really great," he admits, "but on the other hand it's kind of empty."

Empty? "Yeah—it's like Christmas. It's wonderful and all, but the anticipation might be a little more fun, and you still have to take out the garbage the next day. Like, I've wanted this to happen for so long and now it has, but it really hasn't changed anything about my life."

Oh, come on—nothing? For example, I remember walking to a college class two months after Red Right 88, and an icy wind swept down a city street, freezing me, and for a moment I was back at the stadium, and there was that pass, and, oh, if Sipe just hadn't thrown it, the Browns could have . . . oof! I actually bent over and grimaced there on that St. Louis street. Doesn't he get the opposite thing now?

Yep, David says. "Oh yeah. For a good long while afterwards, I would be just puttering around and it would occur to me, 'Hey! The Broncos won the Super Bowl! Hurray!' And it would put a spring in my step for 10 minutes. It was a great mood elevator."

And now he's had his championship—in fact he's had two. He and Joe exchanged hearty handshakes after that first one, but there was very little screaming in the streets, despite my encouragement. Still, David and Joe clearly loved their championship, their fan moment, and I have to say I was happy for them. I'm glad the Browns weren't in the league at the time just the same, but I was happy for them.

Looking back on it now David has something a little unexpected to say. He's glad they won and all, but there's a little something lost, too.

"There are times when I do kind of miss the pathos that there used to be," he says. "I know that sounds kind of insufferable, coming from me, but there was something charming about them when they were never going to win a Super Bowl and that was okay because they were still our Broncos.

"That's why you should sort of treasure that."

I think we already do. And it may be that if the Browns ever do win that elusive Super Bowl, I'll feel a sneaking sense of disappointment, and I'll miss my years of support for them when they were the Boston Red Sox of football.

For the record, though, I'm willing to make the sacrifice.

I Have Raked My Last Leaf

I HAVE FOUR THINGS.

I have a pennant, in Browns colors, of Cleveland Municipal Stadium.

I have a bright orange Browns hat with a brown-and-white stripe down the center and, from an ill-considered period during which it hung on a lamp, melted plastic on its adjustable strap.

I have a brown jersey, bought in 1976, that still fits. I have had to sew the orange and white arm stripes back on several times, but I bought this jersey back in the old days when replica jerseys were still considered articles of clothing, so it is made not of the fashionable—and cheap—mesh of today but of some kind of indestructible polyester. The crinkly white iron-on number has been gone for years, but the jersey itself will last for geologic time.

And I have one of those bobbly-head ceramic guys with his giant, grinning helmeted visage bouncing on a wobbly spring neck. Orange helmet, brown jersey with "Browns" across the front and "Cleveland" on the gold base, the little guy looks every one of his nearly 30 years. My brother has one that he got early enough that the helmet is still white, with a brown stripe—the original Browns uniform—and it's in much better shape. He's also got a Packer, a Viking, a Charger, and, I think, a Steeler, and all are in far better condition than my little orange-helmeted Browns dude.

Scotch tape crisscrosses his helmet, his face, and even his comparatively solid chest, where cracks have spread and progressed to the life-threatening stage, requiring surgery. His face mask is actually only the latest in a long series of unbent paper clips pressed into service, the original long gone. He has a big hole in the base, tape across the back, and a head that is, sadly, at this stage of his life, not only highly elliptical but completely removable.

And yet he exists. His battle scars have come not as the result of any fan petulance. I'm not the throwing-stuff kind of fan, so he's never been flung in disgust or jammed into a drawer in dismay. No, his injuries are those of simple endurance. He's cracked and beaten because he's been around. He's stood atop many a television, taken many a tumble when we jumped around celebrating a score, slid off many a bureau surface when we dropped to our knees pleading against a penalty. He's a simple, unassuming little guy, ill-designed for the rough treatment he's received over the years. After many a moment of passion, he's found himself upside down in a dusty place with a fresh ding in his noggin, and as clear thinking returned I've had to search him out and, still in front of the game, apply new mucilage dressing and tape bandages.

I suppose you could find a better metaphor, but he'll do.

Just as it's those pieces of Scotch tape that make this guy more valuable each year, it's those heartbreaking losses that have tempered our dedication to the Browns. It's the dents that prove the love.

And as I look at him on my shelf among my other gewgaws and the foolishness that builds up over a life, I recognize that he's just not going away.

I tried—I tried so hard. When the team moved I gave up football, and I meant it, and I kept to it. Without those orange helmets, football was wearying, a bloodless exercise in a lifeless game. I spent my Sundays productively, and like many Browns fans I wondered. As Browns Backers clubs saw their members dwindle, we all wondered: how many of us would be back? When the new stadium was built, when 45 new guys came running out onto the field for the first game, how many of us would care? How many of us would leap the three-year chasm and be back, cheering again?

I can speak for nobody but myself. And as for me, I'll be different, but I'll be there. Whatever the magic is, it remains. If we're cheering for nothing more than the color brown, then somehow brown is enough. The heartbreak of the move only gets added to the Drive, to the Fumble, to Red Right 88, to the Warfield trade, to the ousting of Paul Brown and the sacking of Kosar, to all the other bumps and bruises that have defined us as fans over the years, mixing with the victories and the passion to form whatever it is that makes all this Brown so lovely, so lasting.

I can't say that I'm surprised, really—too many Browns fans have described this madness as a love affair that you just can't quit, and I'm not sure that I ever really wanted to. The thing is, now they're back, and now I'm back, and now my Sunday afternoons are spoken for, for good or ill.

I have, at least on Sundays, raked my last leaf, and thank God for the Cleveland Browns.

The View from the Tunnel

A Few Words from Jerry Sherk

I SET OUT in this book to understand being Brown, to figure out what it was, what it is, about those guys in the orange hats that makes their relationship to us so powerful. I talked to dozens of people, and it turns out that if you really want to, you can come up with a kind of recipe for the deepest fan commitment in the nation.

Take one part Paul Brown's class organization; add liberal amounts of farsighted innovation and leadership. Ignore differences in color of ingredients; simply mix. Introduce several of the greatest players in football history, including, probably, the greatest ever. Let rise for eight league championships during three decades of excellence, breeding desperate Yankee-style pride; cool for two subsequent decades of near-miss heartbreak, breeding fierce Red Sox–style pessimistic faith. Place before fans bred to sincere, Midwestern-strength, Great Lakes–style support, then disperse those fans worldwide, mixing fan loyalty with civic nostalgia. Turn up the heat under the town, changing it from a national punch line into a genuine source of international pride.

Then remove the team.

Stand back.

What you've got is the only group of people in the nation who ever demanded their team back—and got it back. What you've got is the only team that ever wanted to come back so badly. What you've got is the Browns.

But even so—big deal. That's only description, and that doesn't quite get to the heart of it. What's at the heart of Brown, of course, is nothing more than pride—and nothing less than love. Like the love of a mother for a child, of lover for lover, it's utterly unique and at the same time utterly common. It's unforgettable and special, yet who can truly describe it? It is what it is because it is, and we all understand it because we live it. Is there anything else to say?

Of course there is. I've had my say, and several fans and players have had theirs. But for the final word, the best description of what this madness is all about, I ended up with defensive tackle Jerry Sherk.

Sherk played for the Browns from 1970 to 1981—his first game was the first Monday night game ever, and he stuck around through Red Right 88 and its aftermath. He started play with Bill Nelson and ended up with Brian Sipe; he played for Blanton Collier and Sam Rutigliano. His first season was the Browns' first after Paul Warfield, and when he left Ozzie Newsome still had nine seasons left. And it turns out that inside the barrel chest of this 250-pound guy from Oregon beats a heart of pure and true Brown.

Sherk sent me a copy of *The Brown Blues*, the video of the journey he and Brian Sipe made to Cleveland for the final game with Cincinnati in 1995. On the journey—and on the tape—he shed real tears, making no bones about his deep affection for his teammates and their fans.

He and I corresponded via e-mail for this book, and he shared his feelings about having been part of something special. He told me how proud he was to be part of the team "in the plain Brown wrapper," how much he enjoyed representing Cleveland when the city most needed it: "The fact that Cleveland was a hard luck town, and the Browns were a quality team, well, it made for a love affair that is still going on. It's a town with a 'hole in its psyche' which fell in love with a team that stood up for it during the tough times, and represented it so well. The Cleveland Browns and the town of Cleveland might be one of the biggest town/team love stories in the 20th century. It's a romance. It's hard-hitting. It's music. From Frankie Yankovic to the Michael Stanley Band."

This is not the type of commentary one expects from a defensive tackle, and when one is fortunate enough to run across it, one thanks the gods for good fortune and gets out of the way.

Jerry Sherk on his feelings for the Cleveland fans: "Overall, the feeling of coming out of the tunnel was fantastic. I also had a general feeling of being privileged to play in Cleveland and in the NFL. Sometimes when I was having a big game, I still felt like a fan, a small boy, surrounded by legends.

"I loved playing for the people. They were my motivation. I related to the people of Cleveland, the underdogs who were fighting for respect. I tried to immerse myself in their emotions, their cheers. As a defensive tackle you had to get wound up every game or you would get eaten alive. I had the philosophy that I was a warrior fighting for respect for the people of Cleveland. I wanted to make them happy and proud to be represented by the Cleveland Browns. I saw the town as kind of depressed, and I wanted to help pull them out of the blues."

Jerry Sherk on the connection between the Browns and their history: "As a player you didn't talk too much about the connection with the town and fans. You may mention it every now and then but you are too busy focusing on playing football. Players tend to not get too deep or too sentimental during their playing days. I think for the most part it was an unspoken respect for the tradition. We didn't sit around the locker room talking about Paul Brown, or Jim Brown. We were too busy trying to make legends out of ourselves. But in our private moments, most of us thought about the tradition.

"For later players this may have changed. Because of the time involved since Brown and Brown, Otto Graham, and all the other greats, the players of the nineties—some of them at least—lost the connection. You will see this on the last part of the *Brown Blues* film after they won the last game. Some of the Browns players are jumping around like it was time to celebrate. They didn't even know they had participated in a funeral. In fact, I saw two of the Browns rookies a year later and they remarked that they were surprised at how the fans reacted at the last game. One of them said, 'Hey, those people were really upset!' Where had he been, I wondered."

And finally, Jerry Sherk—on being Brown: "All the rituals before the game, starting with the nervous energy at the hotel during breakfast. Doug Dieken drinking his 13 cups of coffee. The tingle in your stomach as you took a cab to the stadium. The homely but kind program-seller lady who gave me a kiss during the walk to the locker room. Sitting in my locker I would tear strips of adhesive tape about two feet long. With these strips I would start taping the three outside fingers on each hand. I had dislocated the fingers so many times, they would come out of joint if I didn't give them support. The trick was to tape them tight enough that they didn't come out of joint when I grabbed a jersey, and loose enough that I could grab my opponent. The funny thing was that when I taped my fingers, it would never be good enough until at least my third attempt. I would always rip the tape off at least twice.

"Off to one side of our locker room were steep steps to the tunnel underneath the stadium. These wooden stairs were topped with splinters which had been cultivated by over 20 years of metal football cleats. The tunnel was narrow and fairly steep, and in those days it was lit by a single bare light-bulb about every 30 yards.

"In the tunnel the 45 of us pressed together, and we reached out to the player in front, while being touched by a player or two behind us. We shuffled in that darkness slowly, carefully, with the clomp-clomp-clomp of cleats as the only sound. As we neared the end of the tunnel at the baseball dugout, the light of that opening was almost blinding. The first player out of the tunnel drew the loud cheers of the fans, and the roar echoed up the tunnel and surrounded the rest of us as we continued to make our way forward. As if we needed to get more excited than we already were, that roar made the hair stand up on the backs of our necks, and it made us puff out our chests an inch or two more.

"I will never experience another feeling like that as long as I live. Going slowly down into that dark tunnel, pressed together in unison with my teammates, hearing only the echoing footsteps, feeling powerful and scared at the same time. Now, ready for battle, we quickly rise three or four steps straight up onto the floor of Cleveland Stadium where we are surrounded by 85,000 screaming fans.

"The adrenaline, the pride, the glory. There were no others like us—we were the Cleveland Browns!"

Acknowledgments

I talked to so many people in preparing this book, and my deep thanks go to them all, and my apologies go to any I forget to mention here. I thank Lou Groza, Otto Graham, Jim Brown, Paul Warfield, Mike Phipps, Jerry Sherk, Greg Pruitt, Brian Sipe, Ozzie Newsome, Bernie Kosar, Earnest Byner, and Dick Schafrath for taking time out of extremely busy schedules to help me along. Mike Brown was very kind with his time, and the Bengals' front office went above and beyond the call of duty, as did everyone in the public relations department of the Baltimore Ravens. Chuck Schodowski helped and provided inspiration, as did John Telich, Harold Manson, Jeff Wagner, Bob Grace, John Thompson, Joe Melchior, and a host of other Browns fans past and present. Dan Arthur of the Cleveland Browns front office helped by providing phone numbers when he could, and Dino Lucarelli provided information on Abe Abraham. Barbara Dundon connected me with Otto Graham twice, and Tim Long offered help as both friend and writer. His book *Browns Memories* was a helpful reference, as were *When All the World Was Browns Town*, by Terry Pluto, and *Glory for Sale*, by Jon Morgan. John Moore at the Denver Post helped me locate a key quote. I also thank the Cleveland Press Archives at Cleveland State University for use of the photographs in this book, and Bill Barrow and his staff for help with the photo research.

David Gray of Gray & Company, Publishers, understood this book from the start and took a chance on it, even providing a sensitive edit himself; his entire staff did a great job. Susan Raihofer believed and supported when it would have been easy to doubt and discourage and has become far more friend than agent, though she still deserves a percentage. She read this book and provided marvelous feedback. Michael Singer, Joe Miller, David Menconi, Angela Clemmons, and my mom and dad and brother and sister all read or listened to sections and deeply supported this work. Lisa Pollak and Chuck Salter provided their usual support, and June Spence provided all that and more—listening and reading over and over, offering help, and in all ways simply making life better. I got to interview my friend David Menconi for this book, and from now on I interview only other writers. Catering by Leigh Menconi.

SPORTS - FOOTBALL

Browns Town 1964 / The remarkable story of the upstart AFC Cleveland Browns' surprise championship win over the hugely favored Baltimore Colts. *Terry Pluto* / $14.95 softcover

The Browns Fan's Tailgating Guide / Fun tips from Cleveland's top tailgaters—about where to, when to, and how to do it all, Browns fan style. *Peter Chakerian* / $9.95 softcover

Heart of a Mule / Former Browns and OSU Buckeye player, Dick Schafrath retells many wild and entertaining stories from his life. *Dick Schafrath* / $24.95 hardcover

The Toe / No one played longer for the Browns. Relive the golden era of pro football in this autobiography by Lou "The Toe" Groza. *with Mark Hodermarsky* / $12.95 softcover

On Being Brown / Thoughtful and humorous essays and interviews with legendary Browns players ponder what it means to be a true Browns fan. *Scott Huler* / $12.95 softcover

False Start / A top sports journalist takes a hard look at the new Browns franchise and tells how it was set up to fail. *Terry Pluto* / $19.95 hardcover

SPORTS - BASEBALL

Dealing / A behind-the-scenes look at the Cleveland Indians front office that tells how and why trades and other deals are made to build the team. *Terry Pluto* / $14.95 softcover

The Top 20 Moments in Cleveland Sports Twenty exciting stories recount the most memorable and sensational events in Cleveland sports history. *Bob Dyer* / $14.95 softcover

Ask Hal / Answers to fans' most interesting questions about baseball rules from a Hall of Fame sportswriter. *Hal Lebovitz* / $14.95 softcover

The Curse of Rocky Colavito / The classic book about the Cleveland Indians' amazing era of futility: 1960-1993. *Terry Pluto* / $14.95 softcover

Whatever Happened to "Super Joe"? / Catch up with 45 good old guys from the bad old days of the Cleveland Indians. *Russell Schneider* / $14.95 softcover

Our Tribe / A father, a son, and the relationship they shared through their mutual devotion to the Cleveland Indians. *Terry Pluto* / $14.95 softcover

SPORTS - GENERAL

The Franchise / An in-depth look at how the Cleveland Cavaliers were completely rebuilt around superstar LeBron James. *Terry Pluto & Brian Windhorst* / $19.95 hardcover

LeBron James: The Rise of a Star / From high school hoops to #1 NBA draft pick, an inside look at the life and early career of basketball's hottest young star. *David Lee Morgan Jr.* / $14.95 softcover

Best of Hal Lebovitz / A collection of great sportswriting from six decades, by the late dean of Cleveland sportswriters. *Hal Lebovitz* / $14.95 softcover

Curses! Why Cleveland Sports Fans Deserve to Be Miserable / A collection of a lifetime of tough luck, bad breaks, goofs, and blunders. *Tim Long* / $9.95 softcover

Heroes, Scamps & Good Guys / 101 profiles of the most colorful characters from Cleveland sports history. Will rekindle memories for any Cleveland sports fan. *Bob Dolgan* / $24.95 hardcover

TRAVEL & GUIDES

Ohio Road Trips / Discover 52 of Neil Zurcher's all-time favorite Ohio getaways. *Neil Zurcher* / $13.95 softcover

Cleveland Ethnic Eats / The guide to authentic ethnic restaurants and markets in Northeast Ohio. *Laura Taxel* / $14.95 softcover

52 Romantic Outings in Greater Cleveland / Easy-to-follow "recipes" for romance —a lunch hour, an evening, or a full day together. *Miriam Carey* / $13.95 softcover

Bed & Breakfast Getaways from Cleveland / Great Inn Getaways from Cleveland / Small inns and hotels, perfect for an easy weekend or evening away from home. *Doris Larson* / $14.95 (each) softcover

Ohio Oddities / An armchair guide to the offbeat, way out, wacky, oddball, and otherwise curious roadside attractions of the Buckeye State. *Neil Zurcher* / $14.95 softcover

NATURE & OUTDOORS

Trail Guide to Cuyahoga Valley National Park / The complete guide to Ohio's own national park, written by the people who know it best. *Cuyahoga Valley Trails Council* / $15.95 softcover

Cleveland on Foot / Beyond Cleveland on Foot / Great hikes and self-guided walking tours in and around Greater Cleveland and 7 neighboring counties. *Patience Cameron Hoskins, with Rob & Peg Bobel* / $15.95 (each) softcover

Cleveland Fishing Guide / Best public fishing spots in Northeast Ohio, what kind of fish you'll find, and how to catch them. Directory of fishing resources. *John Barbo* / $14.95 softcover

Dick Goddard's Weather Guide for Northeast Ohio / Seasonal facts, folklore, storm tips, and weather from Cleveland's top meteorologist. / $13.95 softcover

HISTORY & NOSTALGIA

Big Chuck! / Cleveland TV legend "Big Chuck" Schodowski tells hundreds of funny and surprising stories from a lifetime in television. *Chuck Schodowski* / $19.95 hardcover

The Buzzard / A rock and roll radio memoir about the wild days at Cleveland's WMMS from 1973 to 1986. *John Gorman* / $14.95 softcover

Cleveland Rock & Roll Memories / Revisit the glory days of rock & roll in Cleveland. *Carlo Wolff* / $19.95 softcover

Strange Tales from Ohio / Offbeat tales about the Buckeye State's most remarkable people, places, and events. *Neil Zurcher* / $14.95 softcover

Cemeteries of Northeast Ohio / Meet our most interesting "permanent residents" at 120 local cemeteries. *Vicki Blum Vigil* / $15.95 softcover

Cleveland Food Memories / A nostalgic look back at the food we loved, the places we bought it, and the people who made it special. *Gail Ghetia Bellamy* / $17.95 softcover

Cleveland Amusement Park Memories A nostalgic look back at Euclid Beach Park, Puritas Springs Park, Geauga Lake Park, and other classic parks. *David & Diane Francis* / $19.95 softcover

Barnaby and Me / Linn Sheldon, a Cleveland TV legend as "Barnaby," tells the fascinating story of his own extraordinary life. / $12.95 softcover

The Cleveland Orchestra Story / How a midwestern orchestra became a titan in the world of classical music. With 102 rare photographs. *Donald Rosenberg* / $40.00 hardcover

Finding Your Family History / Practical how-to with detailed instructions to help find the roots to your family tree in Northeast Ohio. *Vicki Blum Vigil* / $19.95 softcover

Ghoulardi / The behind-the-scenes story of Cleveland's wildest TV legend. Rare photos, interviews, show transcripts, and Ghoulardi trivia. *Tom Feran & R. D. Heldenfels* / $17.95 softcover

Whatever Happened to the "Paper Rex" Man? / Nostalgic essays and photos rekindle memories of Cleveland's Near West Side neighborhood. *The May Dugan Center* / $15.95 softcover

CRIME & MYSTERY

The Serial Killer's Apprentice / Thirteen true stories about the most notorious unsolved crimes in the last half century of Northeast Ohio. *James Renner* / $14.95 paperback

Amy: My Search for Her Killer / Secrets and suspects in the unsolved murder of Amy Mihaljevic. *James Renner* / $24.95 hardcover

Cleveland Cops / Sixty cops tell gritty and funny stories about patrolling the streets of Cleveland. *John H. Tidyman* / $14.95 paperback

They Died Crawling
The Maniac in the Bushes
The Corpse in the Cellar
The Killer in the Attic
Death Ride at Euclid Beach
Five collections of gripping true tales about notable Cleveland crimes and disasters. Includes photos. *John Stark Bellamy II* / $13.95 softcover (each)

Women Behaving Badly / 16 strange-but-true tales of Cleveland's most ferocious female killers. *John Stark Bellamy II* / $24.95 hardcover

The Milan Jacovich mystery series / Cleveland's favorite private eye solves tough cases in these 13 popular detective novels. *Les Roberts* / $13.95 (each) softcover

We'll Always Have Cleveland / The memoir of mystery novelist Les Roberts, his character Milan Jacovich, and the city of Cleveland. *Les Roberts* / $24.95 hardcover

AND MUCH MORE . . .

Truth & Justice for Fun & Profit / Collected newspaper reporting from 25 years by the *Plain Dealer*'s Michael Heaton. / $24.95 hardcover

Do I Dare Disturb the Universe? / A memoir of race and education, this is the story of a girl who grew up and out of the Cleveland projects in the 1960s and '70s. *Charlise Lyles* / $14.95 softcover

Feagler's Cleveland The best and most talked about columns from three decades of commentary by Cleveland's top columnist, Dick Feagler. / $13.95 softcover

What's So Big About Cleveland, Ohio? 10-year-old Amanda expects to be bored visiting Cleveland—until she makes an exciting discovery. Illustrated children's book. *Sara Holbrook* / $17.95 hardcover